Hiking Guide to

SPOKANE

Your Comprehensive Guide to
Hiking Spokane

Nelson Newman

COPYRIGHT NOTICE

DISCLAIMER

Please note that the information contained within this document is for educational purposes only. The information contained herein has been obtained from sources believed to be reliable at the time of publication. The opinions expressed herein are subject to change without notice.

Readers acknowledge that the Author / Publisher is not engaging in rendering legal, financial or professional advice. The Publisher / Author disclaims all warranties as to the accuracy, completeness, or adequacy of such information.

The Publisher assumes no liability for errors, omissions, or inadequacies in the information contained herein or from the interpretations thereof. The publisher / Author specifically disclaims any liability from the use or application of the information contained herein or from the interpretations thereof.

TABLE OF CONTENTS

INTRODUCTION

OVERVIEW OF THE
SPOKANE HIKING SCENE

Welcome to Spokane, where hiking is more than simply a hobby; it is a way of life. Spokane, located in the center of Eastern Washington, has an impressive network of trails for hikers of all skill levels. Whether you're a native or a guest, the city's natural splendor and different landscapes make an ideal setting for your outdoor experiences.

Spokane's hiking setting combines lush forests, steep hills, and peaceful streams. The region's climate, which has four different seasons, allows you to go trekking all year. From the vivid hues of autumn to the snow-covered paths of winter, each season adds its own unique appeal to the hiking experience. The city's closeness to the Rocky Mountains and the Columbia River adds to its attraction, with a variety of paths that exhibit everything from alpine meadows to river gorges.

Local trails are well-maintained and accessible, with something for everyone. Whether you want to climb a difficult mountain, take a leisurely walk through the woods, or discover scenic lake vistas, Spokane's trails will not disappoint. The surrounding areas are also rich in animals and gorgeous vistas, making each hike an unforgettable experience.

Why Spokane Is an Excellent Hiking Destination

Spokane's popularity as a hiking destination derives from its diversified landscapes and easily accessible routes. One of the most notable features is the variation of terrain. The region has undulating hills, lush woods, vast plains, and stunning cliffs. Because of its diversity, Spokane offers a route for every type of trek.

One of the most distinguishing qualities of Spokane's hiking trails is their accessibility. Many of the nicest trails are within a short drive from the city center, making them perfect for a quick day trek or a relaxing day in nature. The well-maintained routes and good markings make it simple for both novice and expert hikers to navigate the trails without becoming disoriented.

Furthermore, Spokane's outdoor community is active and hospitable. Local hiking groups and internet forums are thriving with enthusiastic hikers eager to share their favorite paths and suggestions. Whether you're looking for recommendations or want to connect with other hikers, you'll find lots of support and friendship.

Another reason Spokane stands out as a hiking destination is its dedication to conserving natural areas. Many of the paths are located within well-managed parks and protected areas that promote conservation and sustainability. This means you can enjoy your trek knowing that the natural beauty you're seeing is being protected and conserved for future generations.

How to Use This Guide

This guide is intended to be a thorough companion for hiking around Spokane, whether you're a beginner or a seasoned veteran. Here's how to make the most of it.

Tailor Your Experience: Use the Table of Contents to get directly to the areas that are most important to you. If you're new to hiking, start with the chapters on essential gear and planning your trek; if you're a seasoned hiker searching for new paths, read the chapter on best hiking trails.

Plan Ahead: Before hitting the trails, read the sections on hike planning, safety, and preparation. These chapters will explain what to expect and how to prepare for various trail conditions and obstacles.

Select the Right Trail: The chapter on top hiking trails in Spokane has thorough information of the greatest trails in the area. Use this area to identify paths that are appropriate for your ability level and interests, whether you're searching for a quick, picturesque stroll or a more challenging adventure.

Gear Up: The important gear and equipment chapter will help you select the appropriate clothes, footwear, and accessories for your hikes. To ensure a safe and comfortable trip on the trails, you must be well-prepared with the appropriate gear.

enhance Your Skills: If you want to enhance your hiking methods or learn new tricks, read the sections on hiking techniques and suggestions. These sections provide important guidance on anything from good hiking technique to dealing with difficult terrain.

Stay Safe: The chapter on safety and preparedness is essential reading. It addresses critical issues such as first aid, wildlife encounters, and emergency preparedness. Knowing how to deal with possible threats will keep you safe on the trails.

Make It an Adventure: The example itineraries are intended to help you arrange treks based on your interests and ability level. Whether you're planning a family getaway or a solo journey, these itineraries offer inspiration and practical information for a great hiking trip.

Respect Nature: The chapter on what to do and what not to do will help you practice proper trail etiquette and protect the ecosystem. Follow these recommendations to leave no trace and help preserve Spokane's natural beauty.

Using this book as a reference will prepare you to go on a range of treks and make the most of your stay in Spokane. Whether you're exploring old paths or finding new ones, this book will help you feel confident and excited about your hiking adventures.

Now lace up your hiking boots, pack your kit, and prepare to explore Spokane's wonderful trails. Adventure beckons, and with this book in hand, you'll be ready to explore the best of the great outdoors.

CHAPTER 1

ESSENTIAL GEAR AND EQUIPMENT

Selecting the Right Footwear

When it comes to hiking, your footwear may make or break your experience. As someone who has spent numerous hours on the trail, I can assure you that investing in the correct hiking boots or shoes is critical. The improper footwear can cause blisters, weary feet, and even injuries, whilst the perfect pair can make your hiking experience genuinely delightful.

Begin by evaluating the terrain you'll be traveling. For steep and uneven paths, robust, supportive hiking boots are excellent. These boots often provide extra ankle support and have thicker bottoms with aggressive treads to improve grip. They're intended to keep your feet safe from jagged pebbles and give stability over uneven terrain.

Lightweight hiking shoes or trail runners are ideal for smoother, better-maintained paths. These are often more adaptable and comfortable, making them ideal for paths with less difficult terrain. They frequently have breathable mesh uppers, which assist keep your feet cool and dry on hot days.

Another important component is fitness. Your hiking shoes should fit snugly but not too tightly. There should be enough area in the toe box for your toes to wriggle while keeping your heel from slipping up and down. I recommend trying on boots or shoes in the late afternoon or evening, when your feet are slightly swollen from the day's events. To ensure an appropriate fit, use the same socks you will use while hiking.

Do not underestimate the value of break-in time. Before embarking on a lengthy journey, try out your new footwear around the home or on small hikes. This method helps to shape the footwear to your feet and avoid unpleasant blisters.

Clothing for Comfort and Safety

Layering is essential in hiking apparel. The weather on the route can change quickly, so being able to shift your gear can keep you comfortable and safe. How to Layer Effectively:

Base Layer: Use moisture-wicking materials, such as merino wool or synthetic textiles, as your first line of protection against the elements. These fabrics wick sweat away from your skin, keeping you dry and comfortable. Cotton is not recommended for this layer since it absorbs moisture and might make you feel cold in lower temperatures.

Mid Layer: This layer provides insulation. Fleece coats and lightweight down vests are excellent alternatives. They trap heat, keeping you toasty while remaining breathable. If you're trekking in cooler weather, pack a thicker mid-layer or a fleece and down jacket.

The outer layer protects against wind, rain, and snow: A sturdy waterproof and windproof jacket is necessary. Look for coats with breathable membranes, such as Gore-Tex, that keep rain out while allowing perspiration to evaporate. Make sure the jacket includes adjustable cuffs, a hood, and ventilation zippers for more adaptability.

For warmer weather, choose for lightweight, quick-drying pants, while heavier, insulated trousers are best for colder temperatures. Convertible pants with zip-off legs can be an excellent choice for changing weather because they allow you to switch between pants and shorts as needed.

Don't forget the accessories. A wide-brimmed hat shields your face from the sun, but a beanie or balaclava provides warmth in chilly weather. Gloves are essential in cold weather; they should be both warm and dexterous. Select lightweight, moisture-wicking socks to keep your feet dry and comfy.

Backpack Essentials

A well-packed backpack might be your greatest companion on the trip. It's not enough to just carry your stuff; you also need to pack it efficiently and have quick access to what you need. Here's a list of items you should carry in your backpack:

Carry extra water to stay hydrated on your hike. A hydration reservoir (or Camelbak) with a hose allows for simple drinking while on the go. Alternatively, a few water bottles will suffice. For longer hikes, consider using a water filter or purification tablets to safely refill from natural sources.

Pack high-energy, light snacks like trail mix, energy bars, and dried fruit. For longer hikes, pack a lunch with non-perishable items such as jerky, nuts, and crackers.

A basic first aid kit should include adhesive bandages, antiseptic wipes, blister treatment, and any necessary medications. It's also a good idea to pack a small knife or multitool for various tasks.

Emergency Items: A whistle, a compact torch or headlamp (with spare batteries), and a basic emergency shelter (such as a space blanket or bivvy bag) are important for unexpected scenarios.

Navigation Tools: Even if you have a GPS gadget or smartphone, carry a map of the region and a compass. These classic tools are dependable and do not require battery power.

Rain Gear: Bring a rain cover for your bag to keep it dry. If rain is forecast, a waterproof bag liner might offer further protection.

Personal Items: Bring sunscreen, SPF lip balm, bug repellent, and any necessary hygiene products. Also, remember to bring a camera or smartphone to record the view.

Pack additional layers, such as a lightweight insulating layer and waterproof jacket, to prepare for unforeseen weather changes.

Navigation Tools: Maps, Compasses, and GPS

Knowing how to navigate is vital for any hiker. While contemporary technology provides strong capabilities, old navigation methods are as useful. Here's a guide on utilizing maps, compasses, and GPS devices effectively:

Maps: A topographic map is vital for comprehending the terrain and planning your journey. It indicates elevation changes, landmarks, and trail junctions. Familiarize yourself with map symbols and contours before hitting the path. Always bring a real map, even if you're depending on technological navigation tools.

Compass: A basic but efficient instrument for direction. It assists you in determining your direction and may be used in conjunction with a map to navigate a certain route. Use a compass to take bearings and align your map to guarantee you're going in the proper direction.

GPS Devices: Smartphone apps provide real-time tracking and route planning. Make sure your smartphone is fully charged before your trek, and include a backup power source if feasible. While GPS is useful, be in mind that it may be less dependable in regions with weak signal coverage or high tree cover. Always have a map and compass as a backup.

Combining Tools: Use many tools for optimal navigation. Start with a map and compass to get oriented and plan your path. GPS allows for real-time tracking and changes. Practice transitioning between these tools dependent on your location and terrain.

Additional Gear for Various Conditions

Depending on the season and the route conditions, you may want additional equipment to guarantee a safe and enjoyable trek. Here's a rundown of the additional gear you could consider:

Winter Hiking Gear: Use crampons or microspikes for grip on snow or ice. Trekking poles can help you stay stable on slippery conditions. Dress in layers, and make sure your outer layer is waterproof and windproof.

Summer Hiking Gear: For hot weather, include sun protection like a wide-brimmed hat and UV-blocking sunglasses. Lightweight, moisture-wicking apparel will help you stay cool. Consider bringing a portable water filter to replenish from streams.

Rain goods: In addition to a rain jacket, a waterproof pack cover is essential to keep your goods dry. Waterproof trousers can offer additional protection during heavy rain.

Night Hiking Gear: Bring a dependable headlamp or torch with additional batteries for night hikes. Reflective clothing or a light stick can aid improve visibility.

Emergency Gear: In rural places, a satellite communicator or emergency beacon can save lives. These gadgets can broadcast distress signals and communicate with rescue personnel if necessary.

You'll be ready for anything the path has in store if you carefully choose and pack the correct gear. Remember, the objective is to strike a balance between comfort, safety, and convenience. With the proper gear, your hiking trips in Spokane will be not only exciting, but also safe and pleasurable.

CHAPTER 2

PLAN YOUR HIKE

Choosing the Perfect Trail

Choosing the ideal path is like laying the groundwork for an unforgettable experience. As someone who has hiked innumerable trails, I can tell you that choosing the correct path may be the difference between an invigorating hike and one that leaves you feeling dejected. Here's how to select the appropriate one for you:

Determine Your Fitness Level: Begin by measuring your fitness and hiking experience. If you are new to hiking or have been out of practice, find a path that is appropriate for your present ability. Look for simple to moderate paths with gradual elevation changes and short lengths. For more experienced hikers, difficult treks with higher climbs and harsher terrain may be more suitable.

Define Your Goals: What do you want to achieve throughout your hike? Are you seeking for breathtaking views, a relaxing walk through the woods, or an opportunity to observe wildlife? Your goals will help you limit down your alternatives. Trails leading to peaks or vistas are perfect for soaking in spectacular views. For a peaceful experience, search for pathways that go through forests or beside rivers.

Consider the Length: Trail length is another important consideration. A short, uncomplicated track may be ideal for a day trip or if you're hiking with kids or less experienced companions. Longer routes, particularly those over 10 miles, may need additional preparation, including as bringing extra food and preparing for stops.

Research Trail Features: Each path has its own distinct qualities. Some may have historical or cultural significance, while others may give possibilities for animal observation or seasonal wildflower blooming. To learn more about the route features, consult guidebooks, hiking websites, and local resources. Reviews from other hikers can also give useful information about what to expect.

Check accessibility: Consider the trail's accessibility. Some trails are in isolated locations and require a journey on bad roads, but others are easily accessible from the city. Consider how far you're willing to go to reach the trailhead and whether you're confident managing possibly difficult road conditions.

Consider Time: Plan your hike according to the time you have available. Make sure to include the time it takes to get to the trailhead, hike the path, and return. Include breaks, picture opportunities, and any extra time required for unforeseen delays.

Understanding the Trail Ratings

Trail ratings are a useful tool for determining what you're getting into before you put on your hiking boots. Understanding these classifications can help you pick a path that is appropriate for your ability level and hiking objectives.

Difficulty Ratings: Most trails are classified as easy, moderate, or challenging. Easy paths are often level or have modest inclines, making them ideal for novices or people who want to take a leisurely walk. Moderate paths may have some elevation rise and difficult terrain, necessitating greater work and stamina. Difficult paths are demanding, with steep climbs, harsh terrain, and lengthy lengths that are best suited to experienced hikers.

Distance and height Gain: Trail difficulty is frequently determined by distance and height gain. Short routes with little height increase are often easier, but longer paths with major elevation changes are more difficult. For example, a 3-mile track with 200 feet of height increase is quite easy, but a 10-mile trail with 3,000 feet of elevation gain is significantly more difficult.

Terrain and Surface: The trail surface can also affect difficulty. Trails with well-kept walkways and smooth surfaces are easier to hike than those with rocky, uneven, or muddy terrain. Some trails may have a variety of surfaces, so be prepared for fluctuations throughout the journey.

Weather Conditions: The trail's difficulty might be affected by the weather. Trails that are passable in dry weather might become dangerous when wet or ice. Always assess the current trail conditions and consider how recent weather changes may affect your journey.

Review Hiker Feedback: Reading evaluations and experiences from other hikers can offer context to trail ratings. Hikers frequently exchange information on trail conditions, unanticipated problems, and overall experiences, which might help you understand what to expect.

Permissions and Regulations

Permits and regulations are critical components of trail planning, ensuring both your safety and the conservation of natural resources. Here's what you should know.

Check Permit Requirements: Some paths, particularly those in national parks or protected regions, need permission to enter. Permits may be required for day walks, overnight camping, or usage of certain trail facilities. Check with the appropriate land management agency or park service about permit requirements and availability. Permits are frequently provided on a first-come, first-served basis, or via a reservation system.

Understand the Regulations: Regulations assist to preserve trails and natural environments. Common rules include remaining on designated routes to avoid erosion, conforming to campground limitations, and observing fire prohibitions. Familiarize yourself with local restrictions to be compliant and help protect the path for future hikers.

Be Aware of Seasonal Restrictions: Some trails have seasonal closures due to wildlife activity, weather, or maintenance work. For example, specific pathways may be blocked in the spring to protect breeding birds, or in the winter due to snow and ice. Before planning your walk, make sure to check for any seasonal closures or limitations.

The Leave No Trace Principles: Adhering to Leave No Trace principles is critical for reducing your environmental effect. This involves removing all litter, not selecting flora or upsetting wildlife, and respecting other hikers. Following these standards helps to ensure that trails remain beautiful and accessible to everybody.

Know Who to Contact: Always carry the contact information for local authorities or trail management in case of an emergency or a query regarding trail conditions. Many parks and forests feature visitor centers or hotlines that provide up-to-date information.

Weather considerations

Weather has a big impact on hiking safety and enjoyment. Preparing for weather requires more than just checking the forecast. Here's how to prepare for different weather scenarios:

Always check the weather forecast before setting out: Check the current weather and prediction for the day of your trek. Pay attention to the temperature, precipitation, wind speed, and any severe weather alerts.

Prepare for Temperature Changes: Weather may change quickly, particularly in mountainous places. Dress in layers so that you may change your clothes as needed. For cooler weather, wear a warm base layer, a middle layer for insulation, and an outer layer for wind and rain protection. In hot temperatures, wear lightweight, moisture-wicking clothes and drink lots of water.

Prepare for Rain: If rain is expected, bring waterproof clothing, such as a rain jacket and a rain cover for your rucksack. Trails can become treacherous when wet, so be cautious and consider using traction aids such as microspikes if the conditions are very slick.

Snow & Ice Considerations: Snow and ice may be especially difficult in the winter and early spring. Make sure you have the proper gear, such as crampons or snowshoes. Check the trail conditions and prepare for limited visibility and cooler temperatures. Always prepare a backup plan in case the situation becomes too risky to continue.

Wind and Sun: Hiking in high winds may be difficult and dangerous, especially on exposed ridges. If high winds are anticipated, consider changing your route to avoid exposed spots. To avoid sunburn and heat exhaustion in sunny conditions, use sunscreen, sunglasses, and a hat.

Emergency Planning: Because the weather may be unpredictable, you should always have a backup plan in place. Know where the nearest shelters or exit points are along your path. Carry emergency supplies such as a flashlight, additional clothes, and a first-aid kit in case of a sudden change in weather.

Preparing for Special Conditions

Certain weather and scenarios necessitate additional planning to guarantee a safe and enjoyable walk. Here's how to deal with some of these specific circumstances.

Wildlife Encounters: Depending on the location, you may see bears, cougars, or snakes. Learn about the local fauna and how to manage interactions safely. Carry bear spray in bear area and learn correct food storage techniques to prevent attracting wildlife to your campsite.

Altitude Considerations: If you're trekking in high-altitude places, keep an eye out for symptoms of altitude sickness including headaches, dizziness, or nausea. Acclimatize by gradually increasing your altitude, remaining hydrated, and doing things slowly. If symptoms continue, move to a lower elevation.

Remote & Backcountry Hikes: Remote or wilderness hikes need special planning. Make sure you have good navigation abilities, as paths may not be well-marked. Carry additional supplies, such as food, water, and emergency equipment, and notify someone of your intended route and projected return time.

Night Hiking: If you want to trek in low-light situations, pack a dependable headlamp or torch with additional batteries. Hiking at night necessitates extra vigilance since obstructions and path navigation are more difficult to spot. Prepare for colder temperatures and poor visibility.

Health and Safety precautions: If you have any medical concerns or allergies, please sure to bring the required medications and notify your trekking partners. It is also advisable to have a basic awareness of first aid and to carry a first aid kit with necessary materials.

Planning your trip with these factors in mind will allow you to negotiate the terrain with confidence and enjoyment. Whether you're heading into known terrain or exploring new settings, good planning ensures that you're ready to face any problems that occur. So strap up your hiking boots, pack your stuff, and prepare to hit the trail—adventure awaits!

CHAPTER 3

SAFETY AND PREPARATION

Risk Assessment and Management

Understanding and managing hazards is an important element of outdoor adventure preparation. If you're not prepared, a pleasant trip might suddenly turn into a challenging scenario due to unexpected weather changes and topographical problems. I've learned from experience that recognizing and controlling these risks is essential for a safe and pleasant trek. Here's how you can accomplish it:

Evaluate your experience and skills: Before you begin, honestly analyze your own experience and talents. If you're new to hiking or want to tackle a more difficult trek, start with something easier. Familiarize yourself with the trail's difficulty, length, and topography. Knowing your limitations and selecting trails that fit your ability level helps to avoid overexertion and accidents.

Analyze trail conditions: Check the trail conditions ahead of time. Check out recent reports for updates on trail closures, obstructions, and other dangers. Weather, erosion, and maintenance work can all cause conditions to change, so having current information is critical. Websites, local ranger stations, and hiking forums are excellent sources of current trail conditions.

Prepare for weather variability: Weather may be variable, particularly in hilly or coastal regions. Check the weather forecast before your trek and be prepared for a variety of scenarios. Bring layers of clothing to react to temperature variations, and pack rain gear if there is a risk of rain. Be mindful of how weather conditions may impact trail safety—ice, mud, or high winds can transform a passable track into a dangerous one.

Know the emergency contacts: Familiarize oneself with the local emergency services and how to call them if necessary. Most hiking locations feature ranger stations or emergency contact numbers that you can use if you have a problem. Keep these numbers on your phone or write them down in your emergency pack.

Evaluate potential hazards: Determine any possible risks along your path, such as steep drop-offs, unstable rock portions, or locations prone to avalanches or rockslides. Prepare by understanding how to properly manage these risks and packing any essential equipment, such as trekking poles for stability or crampons for ice situations.

Communicate Your Plans: Inform someone about your hiking plans, including your route, estimated return time, and any other arrangements. If something goes wrong and you don't return as planned, this information can help rescuers find you faster.

Basic First Aid for Hikers

Even the most well-planned climbs can result in injuries and health complications. Knowing basic first aid may significantly improve how you manage crises on the trail. Here's a list of important first aid skills and supplies:

Treating Blisters: Blisters are frequent during treks, particularly on long or rugged terrain. To cure a blister, clean the area with an antiseptic wipe, wrap it in a blister-specific bandage or moleskin, and prevent bursting it. If the blister pops, clean it gently, use antibiotic ointment, and wrap it in a sterile bandage.

Handling Cuts and Scrapes: Clean any cuts or scrapes with water and use an antibiotic ointment to avoid infection. To keep it clean, apply a sterile bandage or gauze. If a cut is deep or bleeding profusely, apply pressure with a clean towel or bandage to stem the bleeding and seek medical assistance as needed.

Treating Sprains and Strains: To treat a sprained or strained ankle or other joint, use the R.I.C.E. approach (Rest, Ice, Compression, and Elevation). Rest the wounded region, use ice wrapped in a towel to minimize swelling, support the injury with a compression bandage, and elevate it above heart level if feasible. Avoid walking on the damaged region and seek expert medical attention if the injury is serious.

Dealing with Heat and Cold Injuries: In hot weather, look for symptoms of heat exhaustion or heat stroke, such as dizziness, nausea, or disorientation. Move to a cooler area, hydrate, and relax. In cold weather, look for symptoms of hypothermia or frostbite, such as shivering, numbness, or disorientation. Warm the afflicted regions gradually, refrain from utilizing direct heat sources, and seek medical attention.

Dealing with Allergic Reactions: If you have known allergies, bring antihistamines and, if necessary, an epinephrine auto-injector. For severe allergic reactions, use epinephrine as directed and seek emergency medical attention immediately.

Understanding Basic CPR: While it is not particular to hiking, understanding how to do CPR can save a life in an emergency. Take a certified training to learn the fundamentals of chest compressions and rescue breathing.

Transporting a First Aid Kit: A well-stocked first aid pack is necessary. Include things like sticky bandages, antiseptic wipes, gauze, medical tape, blister treatment, tweezers, a thermometer, and any personal prescriptions. Customize your gear to fit the duration of your journey and the demands of your party.

Wildlife Encounters

Meeting animals may be one of the most exciting elements of hiking, but it's critical to approach these interactions cautiously and responsibly. How to Prepare for and Manage Wildlife Encounters:

Learn about the local wildlife: Investigate the sorts of animals you may see on your journey. Understanding their behavior and habitat demands allows you to avoid disputes and handle interactions safely. Bears, cougars, snakes, and smaller creatures such as raccoons and squirrels are examples of common fauna in different places.

Store food properly: Many animal species are drawn to food. To prevent attracting animals to your campsite or trailhead, keep food locked in bear-resistant containers if necessary. Hang food and rubbish away from your campsite, and use animal-proof storage containers wherever possible.

Bear Safety: If you're trekking in bear area, exercise extra caution. Make noise when trekking to avoid surprise a bear, and carry bear spray and understand how to use it properly. If you see a bear, don't run. Instead, carefully back away while still facing the bear. In the unusual case of a bear assault, use bear spray as a last choice and take appropriate defense precautions.

Preventing Snake Bites: In snake-infested places, keep your distance and exercise caution while reaching into cracks or thick vegetation. Wear long pants and boots for extra protection. If bitten by a snake, remain calm, immobilize the damaged leg, and seek medical attention right away.

animals Respect: Always keep a safe distance when observing animals. Avoid approaching, feeding, or attempting to handle animals. Respect their space and enable them to carry out their normal habits without interference.

Wildlife First Aid: If you or someone else is harmed during a wildlife encounter, perform first aid as necessary and seek expert medical attention. Bites or stings from wildlife may need specific care, such as vaccines or antivenom.

Hydration & Nutrition

Proper water and nutrition are essential for preserving energy and general health during your trip. Here's how to stay nourished and hydrated:

Hydration Requirements: Staying hydrated is essential, especially during difficult excursions. Drink water at regular intervals during your journey, rather than just when you're thirsty. On average, you should drink half a liter of water each hour of trekking, although this might vary depending on temperature, humidity, and activity level.

Water Sources: If trekking near natural water sources, bring a water filter or purification pills to ensure the water is safe to drink. Always verify the local standards for water sources, since certain places may have particular suggestions or limits.

Nutrition: Before and throughout the hike, eat meals that are high in energy and easy to digest. Pack a variety of snacks, including trail mix, granola bars, almonds, and dried fruits. For longer hikes, prepare a well-balanced lunch that includes protein, carbohydrates, and healthy fats.

Avoiding Dehydration: Look for indicators of dehydration such as dark urine, dizziness, and headaches. If you detect these symptoms, drink more water immediately and take a break in a shady spot.

Managing Hunger: Eating little quantities of food throughout the trip will help you stay energized. Avoid eating substantial meals just before or during the climb, since they might cause intestinal pain.

Special Dietary Needs: Plan your meals and snacks to accommodate any dietary restrictions or allergies. Ensure that you have appropriate selections and avoid meals that may cause allergic reactions or pain.

Emergency Preparedness

Being prepared for emergencies is a critical component of hiking safety. Here's how to prepare for unforeseen situations:

Create an Emergency strategy: Make a strategy for dealing with situations such as injuries, becoming lost, or inclement weather. Know where the nearest exits and emergency shelters are along your course. Share your strategy with someone who will be looking out for you.

Carry an Emergency Kit: Include goods such as a whistle, multi-tool, first aid kit, fire starter, and emergency blanket. A tiny, portable, waterproof container is great for keeping your stuff organized and secure.

Know How to Navigate: Be comfortable with maps, a compass, or a GPS device. If your technological equipment fail, understanding how to navigate with a map and compass may be quite useful.

Practice emergency scenarios: Familiarize yourself with different emergency circumstances. Practice utilizing your first aid kit, constructing an emergency shelter, and navigating in low-visibility settings. Practice can assist lessen stress and enhance your response to an actual emergency.

Keep Your Devices Charged: Before you go out, make sure your phone or GPS device is completely charged. When going on long hikes, bring a portable charger or power bank. In an emergency, a charged phone can save your life by allowing you to contact emergency services or navigate back to safety.

Maintain Calm and Think Clear: In any emergency scenario, remaining calm is critical. Take calm breaths, appraise the situation, and make reasonable judgments. Panicking might impair your judgment and worsen the problem.

Understanding and preparing for these areas of safety and readiness can help you manage anything comes your way on the path. Remember that hiking is about enjoying the outdoors while being safe, so always prioritize your own safety and well-being as you go on your travels.

CHAPTER 4

HIKING TECHNIQUES AND TIPS

Proper hiking form

Maintaining appropriate hiking form is critical not only for comfort, but also for avoiding injuries and increasing efficiency on the trails. Over the years, I've discovered that proper hiking form makes a huge impact, especially on longer or more difficult walks. Here's an overview on how to keep your form in order:

Posture: Begin with a firm, balanced stance. Stand erect, shoulders relaxed and head up. This position keeps your spine straight and relieves tension on your back. Imagine a thread gently pulling from the top of your head to keep you balanced and centered.

Foot Placement: When walking, keep your feet exactly beneath your hips. This helps to maintain balance and control, especially on rough terrain. Avoid over striding and instead take shorter, more deliberate steps. This strategy decreases the chance of stumbling and makes it easier to cross tough sections.

Core Engagement: Use your core muscles to help stabilize your torso. A strong core helps you stay balanced and prevents strain on your lower back and hips. Consider it a brace that provides support for your body while you move.

Arm Movement: Use your arms to improve balance and rhythm. Bend your elbows to around 90 degrees and swing your arms naturally with each stride. Pump your arms harder on steeper inclines to assist drive yourself forward.

Breathing: Concentrate on deep, regular breathing to maintain your energy levels. Inhale deeply through your nose, allowing your diaphragm to expand, then expel completely through your mouth. Proper breathing improves stamina and lowers tiredness.

Weight Distribution: Distribute your weight evenly on both feet. Avoid leaning too far forward or backward, since this might strain your back and disrupt your equilibrium. To maintain stability while climbing or descending, move your weight slightly forward or backward.

Using Trekking Poles: Adjust your trekking poles to the proper height—your elbows should be at roughly a 90-degree angle when the poles are placed. Use the poles to improve balance and prevent pressure on your knees and joints, particularly on steep terrain.

Effective Trail Navigation

Efficient trail navigation is essential for a pleasant hiking experience and helps you avoid getting lost or wandering off track. Here's how to negotiate trails like an expert:

examine the route Map: Before leaving, thoroughly examine the route map and any relevant trail guides. Familiarize yourself with significant sites, intersections, and the trail's overall structure. Knowing the route ahead of time allows you to anticipate turns and prevent surprises.

Use a GPS Device or App: Although a paper map and compass are useful tools, current technology may improve navigation. Use a GPS device or hiking app to track your whereabouts and follow the trail. Make careful to save offline maps in case you lose signal.

Follow the trail markers: Pay attention to path markings like blazes on trees, cairns (rock heaps), and signs. These indicators help to direct you and show which way to travel. If you're doubtful, double-check your map to confirm you're on the correct track.

Maintain Focus: While it's easy to become sidetracked by the landscape, staying focused on the route ahead is critical. Look for small route signs and variations in topography to ensure you're still on track. This helps to avoid inadvertent deviations and keeps you on the authorized path.

Practice Map Reading: Learn how to read topographic maps and recognize symbols such as contour lines and elevation changes. This talent allows you to predict terrain characteristics and plan your trip successfully.

Check for Trail Updates: Before you go, check for any trail updates or notifications. Trail conditions may fluctuate due to weather, maintenance, or other circumstances. Local hiking forums and park websites frequently give up-to-date information about trail conditions and closures.

Handling Steep and Rocky Terrain

Handling steep and rocky terrain can be difficult, but with the appropriate tactics, you can go through these portions safely and swiftly. Here's how to address them:

Move Slowly and Steadily: On steep or rough terrain, take your time. Quick movements increase the likelihood of slipping or stumbling. Move at a steady speed, carefully planting each foot and ensuring secure footing before taking the next step.

Use Trekking Poles: Hiking poles are especially handy on steep or rocky paths. They offer extra support and assist to distribute your weight more evenly. Use them to improve balance and prevent impact on your knees, particularly on descents.

Concentrate on Foot Placement: On rough terrain, search for firm boulders or sections of solid ground to plant your feet. Avoid treading on loose or unstable rocks that may move beneath your weight. To retain greater traction while climbing, utilize your entire foot rather than just your toes.

utilize Handholds: When climbing steep or rocky portions, utilize available handholds or grip onto solid rocks for support. Be wary of loose rocks that may give way. If you're descending, brace your hands on rocks or trees as required.

Maintain Good Balance: To prevent sliding, keep your weight centered and balanced. When ascending, lean slightly forward and rely on your core for support. To retain control when descending, lean slightly back and keep your center of gravity low.

Take Breaks: Physical activity can be difficult on steep and rough terrain. Take regular stops to relax and collect your breath. This helps to prevent weariness and lowers the chance of accidents.

Tips for Uphill and Downhill Hiking

Hiking uphill and downhill necessitates distinct approaches to preserve efficiency and decrease effort. Here's how to deal with both sorts of terrain:

Uphill Hiking:

Shorten Your Stride: When climbing, use shorter, more frequent steps. This approach helps you keep a consistent beat and avoids pressure on your legs. Avoid extended strides, which can cause tiredness and strain.

Use Your Arms: Pump your arms to assist you go higher. This action engages your upper body while reducing the stress on your legs.

Lean Forward Slightly: When ascending, lean forward slightly to keep your center of gravity above your feet. This stance allows you to retain balance and traction on steep inclines.

Take Deep Breaths: Hiking uphill raises both your heart and breathing rates. Deep, regulated breathing will help you maintain your oxygen levels and prevent weariness.

Take Breaks: Give yourself regular opportunities to relax and heal. Find a level space or a huge rock to rest on and take a few moments to regain your breath and drink.

Downhill Hiking:

Bend Your Knees: Keep your knees slightly bent to absorb the impact of each stride. This approach relieves joint tension and promotes balance.

Lean back slightly: When descending, lean back slightly so that your center of gravity remains over your heels. This stance helps you avoid slipping forward and losing equilibrium.

Use Trekking Poles: Trekking poles can be very useful while descending. They give extra support and decrease the impact on your knees. Use them to stay stable and keep a consistent pace.

Walk With Control: Descend gently and cautiously. Avoid hurrying, as it increases the likelihood of slipping or tripping. Concentrate on placing your feet securely and controlling your speed.

Keep Your Body Relaxed: Avoid tensing up. Tension can make it difficult to maintain balance, increasing the risk of injury.

Staying on the Trail and Minimizing Impact

Staying on the designated trail and reducing your environmental impact are critical for protecting natural areas and having a good hiking experience. Here's how to adhere to these principles:

Follow Trail Markers: Always stay on marked trails and paths. Deviating from the designated route can result in erosion, damage to vegetation, and an increased risk of becoming lost. Use trail markers and signs to guide you and avoid creating new paths.

Avoid shortcuts: Avoid the temptation to take shortcuts or make new trails. Cutting switchbacks or creating additional pathways can lead to trail erosion and ecological damage. To reduce your environmental effect, stick to the set path.

Respect Wildlife and plants: Avoid upsetting wildlife or trampling delicate plants. Stick to designated routes and avoid treading on delicate plants or disrupting animal habitat. Follow Leave No Trace principles to help protect the environment.

Pack Out What You Bring: Carry out all trash and waste, including food wrappers, toilet paper, and other debris. Use designated waste disposal facilities when available, and pack out all waste if facilities are not provided.

Minimize Campfire Impact: If campfires are allowed, use established fire rings and keep fires small. Follow all regulations regarding campfires, and ensure that your fire is fully extinguished before leaving the area. In areas where campfires are prohibited, use a portable stove for cooking.

Educate Yourself and Others: Share knowledge about trail etiquette and environmental protection with fellow hikers.

Educating others helps promote responsible hiking practices and preserves natural areas for future generations.

Mastering these hiking techniques and tips will enhance your experience on the trail, ensuring that you navigate with confidence and respect for the environment. Whether you're tackling steep climbs, rocky paths, or just enjoying a leisurely hike, these skills will help you stay safe, efficient, and mindful of the beautiful landscapes you explore. So lace up your boots, adjust your gear, and get ready to enjoy your adventure with the skills you've learned. Happy trekking!

CHAPTER 5

THE TOP HIKING TRAILS IN SPOKANE

Spokane, Washington, is a hiker's paradise, with a broad choice of trails suitable for all ability levels. Whether you're a seasoned trekker or just starting out, Spokane's trails provide breathtaking scenery and enjoyable experiences. In this chapter, I'll lead you through some of Spokane's best hiking routes, explaining what makes each one unique. Let's have a look at these great pathways.

Trail 1

Riverside State Park's Bowl and Pitcher Trail Overview: Riverside State Park is a hidden treasure in Spokane, and one of its highlights is the Bowl and Pitcher Trail. This path offers the ideal combination of natural beauty and easy trekking, making it a favorite among both locals and visitors.

Highlights:

The walk is called for the impressive Bowl and Pitcher rock formations, offering scenic views. These massive stones, shaped by the Spokane River's power, provide a remarkable visual contrast to the lush green surrounds.

Hiking along the Spokane River provides scenic vistas of pure streams running over boulders, offering a relaxing backdrop to your experience.

Observe local animals, including deer, birds, and the occasional fox. The route also has a rich plant community, including towering conifers and bright wildflowers.

Trail length: 2.2 miles round trip, suitable for a half-day trek. It's well-kept, with a combination of dirt trails and rocky portions, so sturdy shoes are required.

Pro Tip: Visit in the spring or early summer to see the river at its most lively, with lots of water flow and rich flora. For a less congested experience, visit early in the morning or late in the day.

Trail 2

Mount Spokane Summit Trail Overview: The Mount Spokane Summit Trail offers a more challenging experience. This route leads to the highest point in the Spokane region, with amazing panoramic views.

Highlights:

The top offers stunning views of the surrounding valleys and mountain ranges. A clear day allows you to see as far as the Canadian border.

The walk has varied terrain, including woodland trails, rocky outcrops, and alpine meadows. This variation makes the trek more fascinating and highlights the region's different scenery.

fauna Spotting: Higher elevations attract various fauna, such as mountain goats and birds. If you enjoy bird watching, bring your binoculars.

The trail is tough, covering around 8 miles and gaining over 2,500 feet in height. It's best suited to experienced hikers who are up for a challenging climb.

Pro Tip: Dress in layers because the weather at higher elevations changes frequently. Bring lots of water and food to keep your energy levels up during the hike.

Trail 3

John Wayne Pioneer Trail, Spokane to Fish Lake

Overview: The John Wayne Pioneer Trail is a historical trail that runs through Washington, but the segment from Spokane to Fish Lake is especially picturesque and accessible. This walk is ideal for individuals who love a combination of history and environment.

Highlights:

Historical significance: The route parallels the former Milwaukee Railroad, bringing historical interest to your journey. Along the journey, you'll notice vestiges of the ancient train infrastructure.

The section from Spokane to Fish Lake has stunning lake vistas and is ideal for picnics or lounging by the water.

Easy Access: This trail stretch is appropriate for hikers of all abilities and families with children due to its flat and easy terrain.

The trail is approximately 6 miles one-way, with a total round-trip distance of 12 miles if hiked completely. It is well-kept and offers convenient access to the lake region.

Pro tip: Bring a bike if you want to cover more land. The path is especially popular with bikers, who appreciate the smooth ride and the gorgeous views.

Trail 4

Spokane River Centennial Trail Overview: This scenic trail follows the Spokane River from the Idaho border to the city of Spokane. It's a fantastic alternative for people searching for a lengthier, urban path with plenty of natural scenery.

Highlights:

The path offers a unique mix of urban and nature landscapes, passing through parks, historic sites, and along the river.

Enjoy breathtaking beauty, including lovely bridges, overlooks, and tranquil riverfront stretches. The route is especially beautiful in the fall, when the leaves turn vivid tones of red and gold.

The trail is largely level and paved, suitable for strolling, running, or riding. It is open year-round, with well-kept portions suited for a variety of activities.

The path is 37 miles long, but shorter pieces can be chosen to fit your schedule and interests. It's an excellent choice for a day trek or leisurely stroll.

Pro tip: Bring a camera to capture the stunning river views and different urban landscapes. The path also connects to a variety of parks and facilities, making it easy to organize a picnic or rest stop along the way.

Iller Creek Trail

Overview: Iller Creek Trail is a lesser-known treasure that provides a tranquil and pleasant stroll through woodland and open meadows. It's an excellent choice if you want a calmer experience away from the more popular routes.

Highlights:

Serene Atmosphere: The path is less popular, resulting in a peaceful hiking experience. You'll appreciate the tranquility of the woodland and the beauty of broad meadows free of crowds.

The hike offers panoramic views of the neighboring mountains and valleys. The vistas are particularly breathtaking at daybreak and sunset.

The region has a diverse animal population, including deer, birds, and the rare fox. The vegetation ranges from dense woodland undergrowth to vibrant wildflowers in the meadows.

The path is approximately 5 miles round-trip with minimal elevation rise. The trail is well-maintained, although there are some rough areas, so good hiking boots are required.

Pro Tip: Bring lots of water and food, as there are few conveniences along this path. It's also a good idea to have a map or a GPS device, as cell coverage might be intermittent in certain location

Exploring these great Spokane trails will allow you to experience the region's different landscapes and natural beauty. Whether you're looking for a tough climb, a tranquil riverfront walk, or a gorgeous historical trail, Spokane has something for everyone. Each path has its own distinct features and charm, ensuring that your hiking trips in this stunning section of the Pacific Northwest are both rewarding and unforgettable. Happy trekking!

CHAPTER 6

THE TOP HIKING TRAILS
IN SPOKANE

Spokane is a hiker's paradise, with a broad range of routes suitable for all skill levels. Whether you're looking for a difficult climb, a gorgeous walk, or a peaceful escape into nature, Spokane offers a route for you. In this chapter, I'll continue our adventure through some of the greatest trails in the area, highlighting what makes each one unique. Let's look at five more amazing hiking places.

Trail 6

High Drive. Bluff Trail

Overview: The High Drive Bluff route is an urban route with breathtaking panoramic views that provides a wonderful respite from the city without going too far away from society. It's ideal for people looking for a fast trek with spectacular surroundings.

Highlights:

The route offers breathtaking views of Spokane and the surrounding countryside. The high viewing spots offer fantastic photo possibilities, particularly at dawn and sunset.

The trail has stunning overlooks where you may enjoy broad views. These areas are great for moments of rest and reflection.

Historical significance: The trail follows a portion of the original High Drive route, giving historical beauty to your journey. You'll come across historical markers and vestiges of the old highway.

Trail length: 3 miles round trip with modest elevation increase. It's well-kept and open year-round, making it ideal for a quick outdoor trip.

Pro Tip: Because the route is rather short, you might prolong your trek by exploring other connecting trails or having a picnic at one of the overlooks. Bring clothing to react to shifting temperatures, since the weather can change in this altitude region.

Trail 7

Liberty Lake Regional Park: Trails Loop

Overview: Liberty Lake Regional Park has a variety of hiking trails to suit different interests. The Trails Loop is a popular alternative for visitors seeking to explore the park's different landscapes and enjoy the lakeside scenery.

Highlights:

The Trails Loop around Liberty Lake offers stunning lake vistas and opportunity to observe animals. It's a tranquil area ideal for a relaxed trek.

The loop offers diverse terrain, including wooded areas, open meadows, and shoreline trails. This variation makes the trek more fascinating and highlights the park's different ecosystems.

Liberty Lake has a diverse animal population, including birds, deer, and beavers. Keep a look out for these species when hiking around the lake.

The Trails Loop is about 5 miles long with modest elevation variations. It's excellent for hikers of all skill levels and provides a reasonable challenge without being overly demanding.

Pro Tip: The park may become crowded on weekends, so try to go during the week or early in the morning. Bring binoculars for bird watching and a camera to capture the stunning lake vistas.

Trail 8

Dishman Hills Natural Area Echo Ridge Trail

Overview: The Echo Ridge Trail in the Dishman Hills Natural Area provides a challenging and rewarding climb with stunning vistas and a sense of solitude. It is an excellent alternative for individuals who want to immerse themselves in nature.

Highlights:

Remote Hiking Experience: The path provides a sense of peace and quiet away from busy regions. It's ideal for people looking for a peaceful vacation in nature.

Hiking up the Echo Ridge Trail offers stunning views of the Dishman Hills and neighboring valleys. The viewing locations provide superb photographic possibilities and panoramic panoramas.

The trail's rugged and uneven terrain provides a sense of difficulty and adventure. It's ideal for individuals who prefer a bit of a challenge and rough terrain.

The Echo Ridge Trail is approximately 4 miles round trip with moderate to tough difficulty. It's well-kept, but certain portions can be difficult, so plan on putting in some effort.

Pro Tip: Wear strong hiking boots to withstand the rough terrain, and carry trekking poles for added stability. The path is best traveled in the spring or fall, when temperatures are lower and the scenery is more picturesque.

route 9

Ben Burr Trail Overview: This historic urban route offers a unique hiking experience between Spokane's industrial and natural settings. It's an excellent choice for anyone who enjoys mixing urban experience with natural beauty.

Highlights:

The path offers a unique blend of urban and natural landscapes, contrasting cityscapes with peaceful green settings. You'll travel by historic railroads, industrial areas, and gorgeous parks.

Hike through historic landmarks and vestiges of Spokane's industrial history. The route features interpretive signs that give information about the area's history.

The trail passes past scenic parks and green spaces, providing a relaxing retreat from the city. It's an excellent way to explore Spokane's different landscapes.

The Ben Burr Trail is 6 miles long and generally flat, making it suitable for hikers of all skill levels. It's an excellent choice for a relaxing trek or an after-work excursion.

Pro Tip: Because the route is close to various urban facilities, you can simply combine your trek with a visit to a nearby cafe or shop. Bring a map or GPS device, since the route has several access points and linkages to other urban trails.

Trail 10

Mount Kit Carson Trail

Overview: The Mount Kit Carson Trail is an adventure trek with breathtaking vistas and a tough ascent. It's perfect for seasoned hikers seeking a rewarding summit experience.

Highlights:

Summit views: The route climbs to the summit of Mount Kit Carson, offering panoramic views of neighboring mountains and valleys. The top provides a spectacular view of the surrounding.

The trail's steep and hard portions make for a great exercise and a sense of success at the summit. It's ideal for anyone who enjoys a good challenge.

Climb through alpine meadows and wooded areas to witness unusual flora and animals at higher heights.

The Mount Kit Carson Trail is approximately 7 miles round trip with substantial elevation increase. It is advised for experienced hikers who are ready for a tough hike with potentially changing weather conditions.

Pro Tip: Begin your journey early in the day to provide ample time to complete the climb and enjoy the summit views. Prepare for varying weather conditions and carry enough of water, food, and clothes to keep you comfortable on the trip.

Each of these paths provides a unique experience that highlights Spokane's distinct beauty and scenery. From urban activities to isolated wilderness walks, every hiker will find something to love. Whether you're conquering a difficult mountain or taking a calm lakeside stroll, these paths provide great outdoor experiences and opportunities to interact with the gorgeous natural environment surrounding Spokane. Lace up your hiking boots, gather your supplies, and prepare to explore these best routes for an exciting trekking journey. Best wishes!

CHAPTER 7

EXAMPLE ITINERARIES FOR ALL TYPES OF HIKERS

Whether you're a beginner or an experienced hiker, preparing your excursion may significantly improve the quality of your experience. Spokane's diversified geography provides something for every type of hiker. In this chapter, I'll present sample routes adapted to various hiking skills and interests. These can help you make the most of your time on the trails, regardless of the type of trek you want to do. Let's look at some well-planned itineraries that will meet your trekking demands.

Itinerary for Beginners

If you're new to hiking, start with paths that are both doable and fun. The objective is to gain confidence, become acquainted with fundamental hiking techniques, and experience the beauty of nature without feeling overwhelmed.

Morning: Riverside State Park, Bowl and Pitcher Trail

Overview: The 2.2-mile round-trip route is an excellent starting place. The climb is moderate and offers breathtaking views of the Spokane River and amazing rock formations.

Highlights: Admire the beautiful Bowl and Pitcher rock formations and the tranquil river flow. The track is well-marked and not too difficult, making it suitable for novices.

What to Bring: Sturdy hiking shoes, a small backpack with water and food, and a camera to record the breathtaking view.

Midday picnic at Bowl and Pitcher.

Overview: After your trek, have a relaxed lunch by the river. Riverside State Park offers numerous designated picnic sites complete with tables and seats.

Highlights: Enjoy lunch while listening to the river in the backdrop. It's an ideal approach to unwind and appreciate the natural beauty you've just discovered.

Afternoon: Short Walk on the Spokane River Centennial Trail

Overview: The Centennial Trail is a flat, pleasant stroll ideal for relaxing after a more demanding hike. You can select a short part, such as the length along the Spokane River.

Highlights: This trail offers scenic river views and comfortable walking. It's an excellent way to broaden your outdoor experience without putting out too much effort.

What to Bring: Comfortable walking shoes, a light jacket (if needed), and a water bottle.

Pro Tip: Always check the weather before going outside and dress in layers. Bring UV protection, such as a hat and sunscreen, particularly on a sunny day.

Itinerary for Intermediate Hikers

For those with some hiking experience and are ready to tackle more difficult terrain, this schedule will give a satisfying and fun day out. It strikes a balance between a decent workout and plenty of picturesque delights.

Morning: Mount Spokane Summit Trail.

Overview: Start your day with an 8-mile round-trip trek that includes considerable elevation gain and breathtaking peak vistas.

Highlights: Enjoy panoramic views from Mount Spokane. The trek covers a variety of terrain, including woodland trails and rocky outcrops.

Bring hiking boots with adequate traction, trekking poles for stability, lots of water, and energy foods like trail mix or granola bars.

Midday: Lunch at the Summit.

Bring a small lunch to eat at the peak. The sights are worth the extra effort, and a well-deserved rest stop at the summit makes the trip much more gratifying.

Highlights: Enjoy the panoramic vistas while dining. Make sure to bring a blanket or seat cushion for comfort.

Afternoon: Descend and relax at Liberty Lake Regional Park

After descending Mount Spokane, visit Liberty Lake Regional Park for a more relaxing day.

Highlights: Walk around the lake or locate a relaxing location. The park provides stunning lakeside views and an opportunity to relax after a tough climb.

What to Bring: Comfortable clothing, a picnic blanket, and a relaxed mindset to enjoy the park's tranquil surroundings.

Pro Tip: Bring an extra layer and rain clothing because mountain weather may be unexpected. Remember to pace yourself and remain hydrated throughout the hike.

Itinerary for advanced hikers

Spokane has some hard trails for experienced hikers looking for a demanding and enjoyable journey.

Morning: Dishman Hills Natural Area - Echo Ridge Trail • Overview: The Echo Ridge Trail is a challenging 4-mile round trip climb with steep elevation gain and rough terrain.

Highlights: Enjoy the tranquility and breathtaking vistas of the Dishman Hills. The trail's difficult topography lends an element of adventure to the trek.

Bring high-quality hiking boots, trekking poles, water, protein bars, and a first-aid kit.

Lunch at a scenic overlook.

Overview: Enjoy your lunch at a picturesque overlook or trailhead. The views are beautiful and make an excellent backdrop for your supper.

Highlights: Take a stop to admire the views and refuel. A simple and portable supper will be excellent.

Afternoon: Mount Kit Carson Trail.

Overview: After lunch, walk to Mount Kit Carson for a tough 7-mile round trip with substantial elevation gain. This hike offers a challenging climb and beautiful peak views.

Highlights: Experience the alpine flora and spectacular peak vistas. The trail's steep nature guarantees a rewarding experience for experienced hikers.

Pack water, high-energy meals, layers of clothes, and a map/GPS gadget.

Pro Tip: Start early to make the most of daylight, and check the weather before leaving. Prepare for sudden weather changes and keep your gear in good shape.

Family Friendly Itinerary

Hiking with family, particularly with small children, necessitates a delicate mix of enjoyment and reasonable obstacles. This schedule includes a variety of simple hikes and fun activities for a family trip.

Morning: Bowl and Pitcher Trail in Riverside State Park.

Overview: This 2.2-mile round trip walk is suitable for children and offers several intriguing sights.

Children may enjoy the natural features of the river and rock formations. The track is clearly defined and simple to follow.

Bring appropriate hiking shoes, food, water, and a small first-aid kit for minor injuries.

Midday: Picnic and Play

Overview: After hiking, select a picnic location in the park for a family lunch. There are various picnic places with tables and plenty room for children to play.

Highlights: Enjoy a family-friendly outdoor lunch and fun in the park.

Afternoon: Explore Spokane's green spaces.

Visit a local park or green space for a relaxing walk or fun. Riverfront Park is an excellent choice because of its large open areas and family-friendly features.

Highlights: The park's playgrounds and strolling routes make it ideal for youngsters.

Pro Tip: Keep the trek short and fun for the kids, and always carry extra food and drink. Plan regular breaks to keep everyone comfortable and pleased.

Scenic and Relaxing Itinerary

If you want to appreciate nature at a slower pace, with an emphasis on visual beauty and relaxation, this itinerary will take you to some of Spokane's most attractive and serene sites.

Morning: John Wayne Pioneer Trail, Spokane to Fish Lake.

The 12-mile round trip trail offers scenic lake vistas and a level terrain for a relaxing trek.

Highlights include the tranquil beauty of Fish Lake and the historical significance of the ancient train track. The trail's flat surface allows for an easy and peaceful hike.

What to Bring: Comfortable walking shoes, a light jacket, water, and a camera to capture the natural splendor.

Midday: Lunch by the Lake

Overview: Plan a relaxing picnic at Fish Lake. The lake's quiet waters and gorgeous surroundings make an ideal setting for a relaxed meal.

Highlights: Enjoy a dinner while admiring the serene lake views. Bring a blanket and maybe a thermos of tea or coffee for extra comfort.

Afternoon activity: Visit the Spokane River Centennial Trail for a relaxing walk. Choose a small part that matches your slow pace.

Highlights: The route provides stunning river vistas and simple walking trails. It's an excellent opportunity to continue appreciating Spokane's natural beauty without feeling rushed.

What to bring: Comfortable walking shoes, a light sweater, and a water bottle.

Pro Tip: Choose a sunny day for your tour to truly appreciate the outside landscape. Don't forget to bring sunscreen and a light jacket for changeable weather.

Each of these routes is intended to give a rewarding hiking experience adapted to different ability levels and interests. By following these guidelines, you may have a well-planned excursion that increases fun while minimizing worry. Whether you're just getting started, searching for a hard climb, or looking for a quiet day in nature, these itineraries will lead you to some of Spokane's greatest hiking experiences. Happy trekking!

CHAPTER 8

WHAT TO DO AND WHAT
NOT TO DO

Hiking is one of the most enjoyable ways to interact with nature, but there are some things you should and should not do to guarantee a positive experience for yourself and others. Over the years, I've learned a lot about what makes hiking pleasurable and polite. Allow me to walk you through some fundamental techniques and frequent hazards so you can get the most out of each path you encounter.

Must-Dos for a Great Hiking Experience

Plan ahead.

Before you lace up your boots and set out, spend some time planning your hike. Investigate the path, assess its complexity, and evaluate the present conditions. Knowing what to expect can allow you to plan accordingly and prevent surprises.

Research the trail: Check maps, read reviews, and learn about its length, elevation gain, and any hazards.

Check weather conditions: Weather may change quickly, particularly in mountainous places. Always check the forecast before leaving and plan for any changes.

Wear the Right Gear

Comfort and safety begin with the proper gear. Invest in excellent hiking boots, clothes, and other gear appropriate for the path and weather conditions.

Choose hiking footwear with enough ankle support and traction. If you're hiking on a rough route, boots with a more aggressive tread will aid.

Dress in layers to adapt to changing temperatures. Moisture-wicking textiles and waterproof layers are critical for dealing with changing weather.

Stay hydrated and nourished.

Hiking may be exhausting, so staying hydrated and fed is critical for sustaining your energy and health.

Bring enough water for the entire hike. A fair rule of thumb is to bring around two liters per person on a day trek. If you're trekking in hot weather or at altitude, you'll need even more.

Pack energy-boosting foods like almonds, dried fruit, and granola bars. Eating little quantities regularly helps you stay energized.

Follow the trail.

Staying on designated paths helps to protect the natural environment and avoid erosion. It's enticing to forge your own path, but it might have long-term consequences for the environment.

Stick to marked trails. To avoid damaging the surrounding environment and becoming lost, stick to well-established routes.

Respect trail markings. Follow trail markings and markers to stay on course and safe.

Use proper hiking techniques.

Proper hiking practices may make your journey more pleasurable while also lowering the chance of harm.

Consider utilizing trekking poles on steep or rough terrain. They give stability and alleviate pressure on the knees.

Pace yourself. Listen to your body and keep a consistent pace. It is best to take frequent rests than to push too hard and risk tiredness or damage.

Common Mistakes to Avoid

Even experienced hikers can make blunders that compromise their enjoyment and safety. Here are some frequent mistakes and tips for avoiding them.

Overpacking or under packing?

A good trek requires striking the perfect balance between overpacking and under packing.

Avoid overpacking since it might slow down and make hiking uncomfortable. Pack only what you need and leave out everything more.

Under packing: Insufficient packing might cause complications. Make sure you have plenty of drink, food, and proper gear.

Ignoring Trail Difficulty.

Not all paths are made equally. Underestimating the difficulties of a path might cause complications, especially if you are unprepared.

Know Your Limits: Choose paths based on your fitness level and expertise. If you're hesitant, start with the easier trails and work your way up.

Understand trail descriptions. When planning your trek, consider the length of the path, the elevation gain, and the terrain type.

Disregarding Safety Measures

Safety should always be the primary consideration. Neglecting fundamental safety precautions may transform a pleasurable trip into a perilous situation.

Ignore weather warnings: If bad weather is predicted, postpone your hike. Sudden storms and severe temperatures can be dangerous.

Forgetting first aid supplies: Accidents happen, so have a basic first-aid kit and know how to use it.

Disregarding local regulations

Rules and restrictions vary depending on the path and park. Ignoring these might result in penalties or other difficulties.

Obtain Permits: Certain paths require permits or passes. Before leaving, double-check your paperwork and secure any essential permits.

Follow park rules. Respect all posted signs and laws to help preserve natural resources and keep everyone safe.

Trail Etiquette

Hiking is generally a group activity, and following proper trail etiquette ensures that everyone has a nice time outside.

Yielding The Trail

Understanding who has the right of way on the route is critical to sustaining hiker unity.

Hikers: Upward or Downward? In general, hikers traveling uphill have the right of way over those coming downwards. Uphill hikers labor harder and require the right of way to prevent excessive exertion.

Trail users: If you're hiking with a group or encounter bicycles or equestrian riders, make careful you yield and communicate effectively.

Reducing Noise

Excessive loudness may disturb wildlife and other hikers. Instead, enjoy the natural noises all around you.

Quiet conversation: Keep talks at a modest volume and avoid loud music. This contributes to a tranquil environment for everyone.

Respecting wildlife: Reduce sounds to prevent frightening or upsetting wildlife.

Passing Etiquette.

When passing other hikers, be polite and safe.

When approaching someone from behind, use a pleasant greeting like "hello" or "on your left" to avoid surprising them.

Safe Passing: Move to the side and pass without disrupting others' pace or balance.

Maintaining cleanliness.

Leave no trace techniques are critical to preserve the beauty of the trails.

Pack out all rubbish, including food leftovers and used tissues. Please leave the trail as clean as you found it.

Use designated restrooms instead than making impromptu ones. If there are no bathrooms, properly dispose of human waste.

Respect for Nature and Wildlife

Respecting the natural environment and wildlife is essential for responsible hiking. Here's how you can help preserve the beauty of the trails.

Follow the "Leave No Trace" Principles.

The Leave No Trace principles help us minimize our environmental effect.

Follow existing routes to avoid erosion and harm to flora and ecosystems.

Respect wildlife. Observe animals from a distance and refrain from feeding them. Human feeding can hurt animals and disturb its natural activities.

Avoid picking plants and flowers.

While it may be tempting to pick a flower or gather a keepsake, it is crucial to leave plants alone.

Enjoy Plants in Place: Take pictures instead of selecting plants. This helps to preserve the trail's attractiveness for future users while also keeping the ecology balanced.

Understand local flora, including rare or protected plants. Respect any restrictions or standards governing local vegetation.

Respect water sources.

Water sources are important for both animals and humans. Protect them by following these guidelines.

Avoid pollution: Never wash dishes, yourself, or your equipment in natural water sources. Use biodegradable soap away from water, and properly dispose of wastewater.

Camp away from water. Set up your campsite at least 200 feet from lakes and rivers to avoid pollution and maintain riparian ecosystems.

Obey fire regulations.

Fires may pose a serious risk, particularly in dry weather. Follow all fire restrictions to avoid wildfires.

Check fire restrictions. Before starting a fire, check the current fire restrictions in the region. During high-risk times, open fires should be avoided entirely.

If fires are permitted, use designated fire rings and ensure they are fully extinguished before leaving the area.

Following these guidelines can help you and others have a more pleasurable and responsible hiking experience. Good practices not only improve your journey, but also help to maintain the trails' natural beauty for future generations. Respect for environment, fellow hikers, and local legislation ensures that hiking is an enjoyable and sustainable pastime. So, prepare to hit the trails and make the most of your outdoor excursions by following these instructions. Happy trekking!

CHAPTER 9

LOCAL HIKING GROUPS
AND RESOURCES

Hiking activities are best experienced not just alone, but also with a group of like-minded people. Whether you're new to the region or a long-time resident, interacting with local hiking groups and taking use of available resources may significantly improve your hiking experiences. Allow me to guide you through how to identify and connect with these Spokane communities and services, as well as why they may be such an important part of your hiking adventure.

Connecting with the Local Hiking Communities

One of the finest ways to improve your hiking experience is to join the local hiking community. These relationships may lead to new friendships, shared knowledge, and group excursions, all of which enhance the enjoyment of outdoor activities.

Join Local Hiking Meetups.

Meetup groups are a great way to connect with other hikers in your area. Spokane offers multiple active hiking meetings that appeal to a wide range of skill levels and interests. Joining these clubs allows you to engage in scheduled treks, learn from expert hikers, and explore routes that you would not have discovered on your own.

How to Find Meetups: Visit Meetup.com and look for hiking groups in Spokane. Look for organizations with active people who go on frequent walks. Examples include "Spokane Hiking Group" and "Spokane Outdoor Enthusiasts."

What to expect: Meetups frequently feature group hikes, social gatherings, and opportunities to discuss your hiking experiences and insights.

Connect with local outdoor retailers.

Outdoor businesses in Spokane may be excellent places to meet other hikers and learn about local trails. Many of these establishments organize events, workshops, and group treks.

Retailers to visit include REI Spokane and The Trail Blazer. These stores frequently have bulletin boards with information on nearby hikes and activities.

Attend retailer-organized activities like gear demos, clinics, and community hikes. These events allow you to connect with individuals who share your enthusiasm for the outdoors.

Participate in community volunteer projects.

Volunteering for trail maintenance or conservation initiatives is a great opportunity to give back to the hiking community while also meeting new people. Many local groups host volunteer days to assist maintain trails, clean up parks, and conserve natural areas.

Organizations to contact: Contact the Spokane Parks & Recreation Department or the Inland Northwest Trails Coalition. They frequently organize volunteer opportunities and can help you connect with other volunteers.

Volunteering supports your favorite trails and connects you with other hikers who care about maintaining the region's natural beauty.

Attend Local Hiking Events and Festivals.

Local events and festivals are excellent opportunity to meet other hikers and learn about new routes and gear. Spokane features a variety of outdoor activities throughout the year.

Examples include the Spokane Outdoor Adventure Show and local trail-running races. These gatherings frequently include guest speakers, gear merchants, and opportunity to network with other outdoor enthusiasts.

Helpful Websites and Forums

The internet has a wealth of information for hikers, ranging from route maps to professional guidance. Here are some useful websites and forums to help you keep informed and connected.

AllTrails.

AllTrails is a great resource for walkers of all abilities. It provides detailed trail information, including maps, user reviews, and images.

Search for trails based on location, difficulty, and length. User reviews and images might help you understand what to anticipate from a trek.

For extensive trail information and GPS maps, download the AllTrails app or visit their website. It's an excellent resource for organizing treks and discovering new paths.

Hiking Project.

The Hiking Project provides thorough trail information and maps based on feedback from hikers who have been there.

Includes interactive maps, trail descriptions, and user-submitted images. The website also provides information on trail conditions and local sites of interest.

To find trails in Spokane, use the website or app search feature. The thorough route descriptions and elevation profiles are very helpful for planning your treks.

Washington Trail Association (WTA)

The WTA is an excellent resource for trail information, volunteer opportunities, and networking with other hikers in Washington State.

Offers trail reports, volunteer opportunities, and a place for sharing questions and experiences.

Visit the WTA website for trail reports and volunteer opportunities. The forum is an excellent location to ask concerns about specific routes and seek advice from experienced hikers.

Reddit – r/hiking

The r/hiking subreddit is a thriving community where hikers exchange tips, trip reports, and gear suggestions.

Features: Ask questions, exchange experiences, and receive advice from a broad community of hikers.

Join the subreddit to engage in conversations. It's an excellent resource for discovering new routes, gear, and hiking suggestions.

Suggested Hiking Clubs and Organizations

Hiking clubs and organizations play an important role in creating a sense of community among hikers. They frequently plan group treks, educational programs, and volunteer opportunities.

The Inland Northwest Trails Coalition

The Inland Northwest Trails Coalition works to improve and maintain trails in the region.

Activities include trail maintenance, lobbying, and community events. They seek to improve trail networks and encourage outdoor leisure.

To get involved, visit their website to learn about future volunteer opportunities and events. Joining their efforts is an excellent opportunity to help local trails while also meeting other hikers who share your enthusiasm.

Spokane Mountaineers

The Spokane Mountaineers is a group that promotes climbing, hiking, and outdoor adventure.

Activities include group treks, climbing competitions, and educational presentations. They provide a variety of activities, including introductory treks and expert climbing expeditions.

To join, visit their website for membership information and upcoming activities. Participating in their activities allows you to meet with expert hikers and climbers.

Spokane Parks & Recreation Department

The Spokane Parks and Recreation Department is in charge of a large number of local parks and trails.

Activities include community treks, educational events, and volunteer opportunities for trail maintenance.

To get involved, visit their website or contact their office for future events and volunteer opportunities.

REI Co-Op

REI Co-op is more than simply a shop; it's also an organization that promotes outdoor leisure and environmental sustainability.

REI provides seminars, group treks, and workshops on outdoor themes.

Check the events calendar for local treks and instructive seminars. Joining their workshops and activities is a terrific opportunity to acquire new skills and connect with other outdoor enthusiasts.

Washington Trail Association (WTA)

In addition to being an invaluable resource, the WTA sponsors a variety of hiking-related events and advocacy campaigns.

Activities include trail maintenance, environmental advocacy, and educational programs.

Get Involved: Become a member, volunteer on trail maintenance days, and attend instructional courses. It's a terrific way to help preserve the trails while also connecting with other hikers.

Connecting with local hiking communities, using internet tools, and joining hiking clubs and organizations will help you expand your hiking experiences and build vital relationships with other hikers. Whether you're seeking for assistance, organizing group treks, or simply sharing your love of the outdoors, these tools can help you make the most of your experiences in Spokane. So, get engaged, remain informed, and reap the numerous benefits of being a member of the thriving hiking community. Best wishes!

CHAPTER 10

SEASONAL HIKES IN
SPOKANE

Hiking in Spokane provides a wide variety of experiences throughout the year, with each season providing its own set of difficulties and benefits. Spokane's natural beauty varies seasonally, from blossoming pathways in the spring to tranquil snow-covered views in the winter. As an experienced hiker, I've discovered that each season necessitates a unique strategy and preparation to ensure a safe and pleasurable excursion. Let's go over everything you need to know for each season so you can take advantage of every hiking opportunity Spokane has to offer.

Spring Hiking Tips

Spring in Spokane is a season of regeneration and development, with wildflowers blossoming and the landscape reviving after winter. However, it has its own set of considerations.

Watch out for muddy trails.

Spring rains and melting snow may create muddy conditions on the trails. While the warmer weather is appealing, the paths may be quite slick.

Invest in waterproof hiking boots with excellent traction. Mud can rapidly transform a track into a treacherous mess, so water-resistant footwear are important.

Trail Etiquette: Walk in the mud as little as possible to reduce trail damage. Stick to the trail's middle and avoid creating new pathways.

Be prepared for variable weather.

Spring weather in Spokane may be unpredictable, with bright days and surprise rain showers.

Dress in layers to accommodate for weather fluctuations. Stay comfortable with a moisture-wicking base layer, an insulating middle layer, and a waterproof upper layer.

Pack a lightweight and breathable rain jacket. Even if the weather prediction appears to be clear, it is always a good idea to be prepared for unexpected rains.

Enjoy the Blooming Flora.

Spring is one of the greatest seasons to see Spokane's wildflowers and lush flora.

Wildlife viewing: Keep a look out for wildlife that is awakening from its winter hibernation. You could see deer, elk, or other bird species. To prevent upsetting them, always observe from a safe distance.

Flora identification: Bring a wildflower guide with you to identify the beautiful blossoms. It's an excellent method to improve your hiking experience while learning about the local flora.

Check the trail conditions.

Spring is an excellent season to go hiking, but certain paths, particularly those at higher elevations, may still be covered in snow or ice.

Trail reports: Before you go, verify the trail conditions and reports. Local hiking forums, park websites, and applications such as AllTrails can give current information.

Summer Hiking Tips.

Summer provides pleasant weather and longer days, making it excellent for lengthy excursions and exploration. However, the heat and possibility for flames necessitate cautious planning.

Start early to beat the heat.

Summer temperatures in Spokane may increase dramatically, making early morning treks more enjoyable.

Start your hike early to avoid the heat of the day. This also allows you to take advantage of the cooler early weather and explore quieter paths.

For sun protection, wear a wide-brimmed hat, sunglasses, and apply sunscreen daily. Sun protection is critical to avoiding sunburn and heat fatigue.

Stay hydrated.

The summer heat may easily dehydrate you, especially on lengthy hikes.

Bring lots of water and drink often during your hike. A decent rule of thumb is to drink around half a liter for every hour of moderate exertion.

Use a hydration pack with a built-in water reservoir and hose for convenient drinking on the go.

Prepare for Wildfire Risks.

Summer is wildfire season, so be mindful of the hazards and limits.

Check for fire bans or restrictions before going out. Follow all rules to avoid wildfires and preserve the natural ecosystem.

Be Fire Aware: Avoid using open flames and ensure campfires are fully extinguished before leaving the site.

Select the Right Trails.

Some pathways may be particularly susceptible to heat or fire threats.

Choose paths with shady sections or higher altitudes to remain cool. Trails around rivers and lakes might provide some relief from the heat.

When planning a longer trek, pick routes with lots of water sources and covered spaces for breaks.

Fall Hiking Tips.

Fall is a lovely season in Spokane, with crisp air and bright autumn colors altering the landscape. It's a season that needs cautious planning as temperatures decrease and days shorten.

Dress in layers.

Fall weather can range from mild mornings to warm afternoons and frigid evenings.

Layering: Wear layers that may be added and removed as required. Begin with a moisture-wicking base layer, then add an insulating layer and finish with a wind-resistant jacket.

Bring additional warm clothing for trekking later in the day, since temperatures can swiftly drop.

Enjoy the fall foliage.

Autumn is known for its beautiful foliage. Hiking in Spokane at this season provides breathtaking vistas of multicolored foliage.

Plan your hikes during peak foliage season for the greatest colors. Typically, the last two weeks of October are when the leaves are the most vivid.

Camera ready: Don't forget your camera or smartphone to capture the breathtaking fall scenery. The fall hues provide excellent picture opportunity.

Prepare for shorter days.

As daylight hours diminish, it is critical to schedule hikes carefully.

Start treks early for optimal daylight hours. Check the sunset hours and schedule your return so you arrive before dark.

Carry a headlamp or flashlight for extended hikes in low-light circumstances.

Be aware of potential fall hazards.

Fall weather may provide its own set of challenges, such as slick leaves and lower temperatures.

Be aware of slippery leaves and muddy places along the trail. To avoid sliding, adjust your speed and monitor your stride.

Bring gloves and a hat for cold weather trekking, especially at higher elevations.

Winter Hiking Tips

Winter hiking in Spokane is a tranquil and scenic experience, complete with snow-covered landscapes and fresh air. However, it necessitates additional planning and safeguards.

Dress for cold weather.

Winter hiking necessitates correct layering to be warm and dry.

Use thermal base layers to wick moisture away from the body. Wool and synthetic fabrics are ideal for staying warm and dry.

Use an insulating layer, like a fleece or down jacket, to maintain body heat. A decent windproof and waterproof outer layer will keep you safe from the elements.

Prepare for Snow and Ice.

Snow and ice create distinct problems that necessitate particular equipment.

Snow shoes: If you're trekking in heavy snow, snowshoes might help you disperse your weight and avoid sinking too deep.

Ice axes and crampons. If you're tackling steep or challenging terrain in icy weather, consider wearing crampons and carrying an ice axe.

Prepare for shorter daylight hours.

Winter days are shorter, so schedule your hikes to maximize daylight.

Start your hikes early to optimize daylight hours. Always be aware of sunset hours and plan your return appropriately.

Bring a dependable light and additional batteries for night hikes.

Be Safe in Cold Conditions

Winter circumstances may be severe, therefore safety is a priority.

Raise awareness about hypothermia. Be mindful of the symptoms of hypothermia and frostbite. Symptoms include shivering, disorientation, numbness, and slurred speech. If you or someone in your group shows these symptoms, seek warmth right away.

Emergency kit: Carry an emergency kit that includes a first-aid kit, fire starting supplies, and high-energy foods. In an emergency, these goods can save lives.

Assess Trail Conditions and Avalanche Risks

Winter paths may be impacted by snow conditions and avalanche dangers.

Trail reports: Before venturing out, check the local trail conditions and avalanche warnings. Websites such as the Northwest Avalanche Center offer useful information about snow and avalanche hazards.

Avalanche safety: If you're trekking in avalanche-prone terrain, bring avalanche safety gear such as a beacon, probe, and shovel, and attend an avalanche safety course if required.

Hiking in Spokane throughout the seasons provides a rich and varied experience, with each season revealing new features of the natural environment. By planning for the unique difficulties and possibilities that each season presents, you'll be able to take advantage of everything Spokane's trails have to offer all year. Whether it's the blooming beauty of spring, the sunny adventures of summer, the brilliant hues of fall, or the tranquil snow-covered vistas of winter, each season has its own set of benefits. So, lace up your boots, embrace the season, and head out to explore Spokane's stunning trails. Happy trekking!

CHAPTER 11

HIKING WITH PETS

Hiking with pets, particularly dogs, may turn an ordinary trek into an amazing adventure. They provide energy, passion, and a sense of playfulness to the route. I've had the pleasure of exploring numerous trails with my four-legged companions over the years, and I've learned a lot about how to make these trips pleasurable and safe for both pets and their owners. Let's go over the ins and outs of hiking with pets, from locating pet-friendly paths to assuring their safety on the hike.

Pet-Friendly Trails

Finding the ideal path for you and your pet is critical to a successful hiking adventure. Fortunately, Spokane has numerous pet-friendly paths that welcome canine friends.

Researching Pet-Friendly Trails

Before venturing out, it's critical to investigate routes that allow pets and understand their individual rules.

Local resources, such as AllTrails, Hiking Project, and hiking forums, can help find pet-friendly paths. Look for filters or tags that say pets are allowed.

Read trail reports from hikers with pets. These assessments can give information about trail conditions, leash rules, and potential risks for dogs.

Popular Pet-Friendly Trails in Spokane.

Here are some Spokane trails that are known to be pet-friendly:

Riverside State Park welcomes dogs on its many pathways. The Bowl and Pitcher Trail, with its stunning vistas of the Spokane River, is an excellent choice. Just make sure your dog behaves properly around other hikers and nature.

The Fish Lake Trail is popular among pet owners due to its stunning lake vistas and level terrain, making it accessible to pets of all sizes and ages.

Palisades Park offers panoramic vistas and modest pathways, making it ideal for hiking with dogs. The pathways here are normally well-kept and provide several possibilities for your pet to explore.

Trail Rules and Etiquette.

Understanding and following trail regulations helps to guarantee a positive experience for everybody.

Most trails require dogs to be on leashes. Even if your dog is well-trained, keeping them on a leash prevents them from running away or harming animals.

Limit leash length to six feet. This provides you control while giving your dog the opportunity to explore.

Trail Etiquette: Be considerate to other hikers. Some people may be afraid of dogs or suffer from allergies. Keep your dog close to you and make sure they behave nicely with others.

Tips for Hiking With Dogs

To ensure the comfort and safety of your dog when hiking, you need prepare ahead of time. Here are some useful recommendations to make your hike more pleasurable for both you and your pet.

Prepare your dog.

Just like you would prepare for a hike, so should your dog.

Ensure your dog is in good physical condition before trekking. Regular walks or runs will improve their stamina.

Training: Basic obedience training is required. Commands like as "come," "stay," and "leave it" may be quite useful on the path.

Socialization: Expose your dog to various surroundings and scenarios to increase their comfort among humans and animals.

Pack essentials for your dog.

Bring everything your dog requires to remain happy and healthy on the trail.

Carry enough water for yourself and your dog in a bowl. A collapsible bowl is useful for giving water breaks.

Pack your dog's favorite treats or meals for lengthy hikes to keep them energized.

Use waste bags to clean up after your dog. Carry garbage bags and properly dispose of them in specified bins, or pack them out if there is no bin accessible.

Prepare a first-aid kit with bandages, antiseptic wipes, and tweezers for minor injuries or tick removal.

Comfort and safety on the trail.

Your dog's comfort and safety are critical on a hike.

Regularly inspect your dog's paws for wear or damage. Consider using dog booties on difficult or hot terrain.

Use a cooling vest to keep your dog comfortable during hot weather. These vests employ specialized materials to assist control their body temperature.

For cold weather treks, make sure your dog has a warm jacket. This is especially crucial for tiny and short-haired breeds.

Rest and Hydration Breaks.

Frequent pauses are necessary to keep your dog hydrated and relaxed.

Take breaks every 30-45 minutes to allow your dog to relax, drink water, and inspect their paws.

Provide pauses in shady locations, especially on warm days.

Safety Tips for Pets

Keeping your pet safe is critical for a good hike. There are various things to bear in mind to avoid accidents and health problems.

Watch out for heat stroke.

Heatstroke is a severe concern, especially during warm weather.

Signs of heatstroke: Look for signs of excessive panting, drooling, disorientation, or lethargy. If you observe any of these symptoms, transport your dog to a cooler area and administer water right away.

Cooling methods: Use a moist towel or a cooling garment to assist them lower their body temperature. Consult a veterinarian if their condition does not improve promptly.

Be aware of wildlife.

Wildlife interactions might be harmful to your pet.

Wildlife hazards: Keep your dog on a leash to avoid chasing or upsetting wildlife. Animals such as deer and bears might respond unexpectedly.

Prevent tick and flea infestations. Use tick and flea prevention products, as ticks may spread infections such as Lyme disease. After the trek, check your dog for ticks, particularly if they were in tall grass.

Protect from injuries.

Injuries can happen on the path, so prepare.

Paw injuries: Sharp rocks, thorns, and uneven terrain can all hurt your dog's paws. Check their paws frequently and apply booties if required.

Understand basic first aid practices for dogs. Understanding how to treat cuts, scratches, and other minor injuries may make a significant impact.

Watch for dehydration.

Dehydration poses a problem, particularly on longer walks.

Signs of dehydration include dry gums, lethargy, and dark urine. Ensure that your dog drinks water at regular intervals throughout the hike.

Avoid overexertion.

Hiking should be fun for your dog, not a test of endurance.

Pace: Maintain a comfortable speed for your dog. If they appear exhausted or falling behind, it is time for a rest.

Adjust distance: Adjust the duration and complexity of your hike to meet your dog's fitness level. Gradually increase their trekking distance to improve stamina.

Hiking with your pet may help you form lasting memories and strengthen your relationship with him or her. By selecting pet-friendly paths, prepping your dog for the trek, and considering their safety and comfort, you can guarantee that both of you have a pleasant and happy time. So, gear up, leash up, and hit the trails with your favorite companion—a whole world of adventure awaits you both. Happy trekking with your four-legged companion!

CHAPTER 12

FAMILY HIKING
ADVENTURES

Hiking with your family is a terrific opportunity to spend quality time together, make lifelong memories, and introduce youngsters to the delights of nature. As an experienced hiker, I've had the pleasure of accompanying my family on several trips, and I've learned a lot about how to make these walks entertaining and safe for everyone, especially the younger ones. In this chapter, I'll provide advice and insights on how to organize family-friendly treks, prepare your children for the path, and secure the safety of the entire family.

Kid-Friendly Trails

Choosing the correct path is critical while hiking with children. You want a trail that is enjoyable, easy, and safe for young walkers. Here are some considerations and trail recommendations in and around Spokane.

Factors To Consider

When choosing a path for a family trek, consider the following:

Choose shorter treks with mild terrain. Children can tire fast, so a route that is excessively lengthy or difficult may cause dissatisfaction. For smaller kids, aim for hikes of 2-4 miles round trip.

Interesting trail elements, such as streams, waterfalls, or beautiful vistas, can captivate youngsters. Look for routes that have interacting components, such as wildlife or unusual rock formations.

Ensure the route is accessible and not too steep. A gradual gradient or level trail is perfect for young children or first-time hikers.

Recommended Kid-Friendly Trails in Spokane

Here are several family-friendly paths that provide a combination of simplicity and adventure: • Riverside State Park's Bowl and Pitcher Trail, a 2.5-mile circle with spectacular vistas of the

Spokane River and a unique rock formation. The trail is largely flat, with a few modest inclines, making it suitable for children. There are many places to stop and explore along the road.

Green Bluff routes: Located northeast of Spokane, Green Bluff has a selection of short, picturesque routes. The paths are typically simple and provide stunning views of countryside and seasonal fruit orchards. It's an ideal location for a leisurely trek with small children.

The 1.5-mile Spokane Falls Community College Trail is ideal for families. It's relatively flat and offers stunning views of Spokane Falls. The trailhead is easily accessible, and the route is well-maintained, making it ideal for families with strollers.

Trail Features for Kids.

When hiking with kids, seek for pathways that include:

Trails featuring interactive elements, such as little streams, animals, or fascinating rock formations, may engage youngsters and enhance their hiking experience.

Designated rest places or picnic locations on trails promote relaxation and reduce weariness. These areas can also be used for a snack or a quick break.

Ensure trail safety by removing risks such as steep drop-offs and slippery parts. Look for clearly defined trails and read current reviews or trail conditions.

Preparing Children for Hiking

Getting kids ready for a trek entails more than simply selecting a track. It's about ensuring they're eager, equipped, and ready for the journey ahead.

Gear & Clothing.

Proper equipment and clothes are required for a good hiking experience.

Ensure your youngster has sturdy, well-fitting hiking shoes or boots. They should offer adequate traction and support to avoid blisters and injuries.

Dress your youngster in moisture-wicking layers. Avoid cotton, since it might become moist and unpleasant. Instead, use breathable, quick-drying materials. Depending on the weather, bring extra clothes, including a waterproof jacket if necessary.

A tiny, child-sized backpack may be both entertaining and functional. Allow them to bring a few personal items, such as a water bottle, snacks, and a tiny first-aid kit. Keep their pack light to reduce tiredness.

Motivating Enthusiasm

Making the trek enjoyable and interesting might help increase excitement and reduce complaints.

Involve your kid in the planning process. Allow them to choose some of the food or their hiking gear. This engagement may improve their excitement for the hike.

Make the hike fun by incorporating games and challenges. Scavenger hunts, "I Spy" activities, and counting different sorts of animals may all add to the enjoyment of the journey.

Positive reinforcement: Praise and motivate your youngster during the hike. Celebrate accomplishments and development to keep their spirits up.

Physical preparation.

Ensure that your youngster is physically prepared for the hike.

Practice Hiking: Take your youngster on shorter, easier excursions to help them develop stamina and become accustomed to the notion of trekking. Gradually increase the distance as they get more comfortable.

Encourage frequent physical activity to improve endurance. Biking, swimming, and even playing in the park can help kids prepare for longer trips.

Hydration & Nutrition

Proper water and nutrition are essential for keeping your youngster energetic and comfortable.

Encourage your youngster to drink water regularly. Dehydration can cause weariness and pain, so drink often throughout the trek.

Pack a range of healthful foods to increase energy levels. Trail mix, bananas, granola bars, and crackers are excellent choices. Avoid too sweet foods, which can cause energy collapses.

Safety Tips for Family Hikes

When hiking with children, safety is the most important consideration. Here's how to plan a safe and pleasant trek for the entire family.

Plan and prepare.

Proper planning can help to avoid many possible difficulties on the path.

Research trail conditions before setting out. Check that it is acceptable for the ages and fitness levels of everyone in your group.

Check the weather forecast and dress accordingly. Be prepared for changes in weather and bring extra clothes or rain gear if needed.

Carry a basic first-aid kit and understand how to use it. Include bandages, antiseptic wipes, and a tiny flashlight. Bring along a map, compass, or GPS device in case you need to navigate.

Supervision.

Constant monitoring guarantees that your children are safe and enjoy the hike.

Stay together: Keep your group together and maintain a consistent pace. Keep smaller children within sight at all times and prevent allowing them to walk off.

Teach Trail Safety: Teach your children to follow defined pathways, avoid upsetting wildlife, and listen to directions.

Know Your Limits.

Be realistic about your family's trekking ability.

Pace: Maintain a comfortable pace for everyone, particularly the youngest ones. Take regular stops to relax and enjoy your surroundings.

Turn around if needed. If the trek gets too difficult or your youngster exhibits indications of weariness or discomfort, do not hesitate to return early. It's preferable to shorten the hike than to push too hard.

First Aid and Emergencies

Be prepared to deal with minor injuries or crises on the route.

Injuries: Familiarize yourself with basic first-aid methods and be prepared to treat minor injuries such as cuts and scratches.

Make an emergency contact list and plan accordingly. Make sure you have a fully charged cell phone and know the location of the nearest trailhead or access point.

Teach respect for nature.

Instilling appreciation for nature promotes a great hiking experience and encourages environmental care.

Teach your children to follow the Leave No Trace guidelines. This includes removing all litter, remaining on authorized trails, and avoiding selecting flora or disturbing wildlife.

Respect wildlife by viewing from a safe distance and refraining from feeding them. This protects both the animals and your family.

Hiking with your entire family, including youngsters, may be a very gratifying experience. By selecting the appropriate paths, preparing correctly, and assuring safety, you can create an environment in which everyone can appreciate the adventure and beauty of nature. Remember that the purpose is to have fun, explore, and create memories together. So, get ready, gather your family, and hit the trails—there's a whole world of adventure waiting for you. Happy family trekking!

CHAPTER 13

SOLO HIKING TIPS

Solo hiking is an extremely intimate and fulfilling experience. There's something really pleasant about being alone in nature, lost in your thoughts and surrounded by wildness. Over the years, I've walked innumerable routes on my own and learned a lot about how to make solo treks both fun and safe. In this chapter, I'll provide fundamental solo hiking techniques, with an emphasis on safety, path selection, and navigation.

Safety precautions for solo hikers

When hiking alone, safety is the most important consideration. Solo hiking, as opposed to group treks, necessitates extreme caution and planning. Here are some essential safety precautions to guarantee a safe and pleasurable solo hiking trip.

Plan ahead.

Before embarking on any journey, careful planning is essential.

Research and select a path that suits your skill level and physical fitness. Look for information about the trail's length, complexity, and any hazards. Websites like AllTrails and local hiking forums might give useful information.

Inform someone. Always tell a buddy or family member about your trekking plans. Provide them with information about your route, approximate return time, and contact information. This way, someone will know where you are and may notify authorities if you do not return as scheduled.

Carry Essential Gear When trekking alone, proper gear is crucial. Here's a list of essentials to pack:

Navigation tools: A map, compass, and GPS gadget are essential for remaining on track. Make sure you know how to use them and have a backup battery for electrical equipment.

First-aid kit: A well-stocked first-aid kit should have bandages, antiseptic wipes, pain killers, and any personal prescriptions. Be familiar with basic first-aid techniques.

Emergency supplies: Bring a whistle, a multitool, a torch or headlamp, and additional batteries. These things are essential for calling for help or dealing with unforeseen occurrences.

Be aware of your surroundings.

Staying aware might help you avoid potential hazards.

Stay on marked trails. To prevent becoming lost, always stick to well defined pathways. Pay attention to path markers and blazes.

Keep an eye out for weather changes: Keep an eye on the weather and be ready for any unexpected changes. Bring rain gear and additional clothes to keep comfortable in changing weather conditions.

Trust your instincts.

When hiking alone, your intuition may be really useful.

Trust your instincts when something doesn't seem right. It's best to err on the side of caution when encountering a change in weather, a weird noise, or an unknown section of the route.

Avoid risky situations. Do not take needless risks. Avoid unstable terrain, harmful fauna, and circumstances that may compromise your safety.

Know Your Limits.

A safe solo trek requires an understanding of and respect for one's boundaries.

Pace yourself: Hike at a speed that seems comfortable for you. Avoid overexertion and pay attention to your body's cues.

Know when to turn back: If you experience difficulties or feel sick, don't hesitate to return. It's preferable to shorten a hike than to push through and jeopardize your safety.

Finding the Best Trails for Solo Hiking

Choosing the appropriate path is critical to a successful solo hiking adventure. You want a path that is both fun and manageable for solo trekking. Here's how you may choose the ideal paths for solo hiking.

Evaluate trail difficulty.

Choose paths that match your hiking expertise and physical condition.

Beginner trails: If you're new to solo hiking, start with short, easy paths. Look for pathways with mild terrain and obvious markers.

Intermediate and advanced trails: For more experienced hikers, select paths with moderate to difficult terrain. Make sure you're prepared for the challenge level and have the proper abilities and equipment.

Consider trail traffic.

The volume of traffic on a path might affect your solitary hiking experience.

Popular trails have more foot traffic, making them safer and simpler to traverse. However, they may be less tranquil and overcrowded.

For seclusion, choose less-traveled trails. These can provide a more relaxing experience, but they may need additional caution and preparation.

Look for trail features.

Trails with intriguing characteristics might help you enjoy your solo hiking trip.

Trails with picturesque views, waterfalls, or unusual geological formations can enhance your hiking experience.

Wildlife Observation: Choose routes in regions with diverse animal and bird life.

Check trail conditions.

Before you go, check the trail's current conditions.

Trail reports: Seek out recent trail reports or updates to ensure the path is in good shape and free of closures or dangers.

Weather conditions: Consider the weather prediction and how it can impact trail conditions. Some pathways may become slick or treacherous under rainy or icy weather.

Assess accessibility.

Ensure that the trailhead is accessible and convenient for solitary hiking.

Trailhead Location: Choose routes with convenient trailheads and plenty of parking. If you're trekking in a distant place, be sure you're okay with the amount of isolation.

Navigation and Tracking Alone

When hiking alone, charting and recording your route is critical to staying on track and finding your way back. Here's how to successfully manage and log your solo hike.

Use the Navigation Tools.

A variety of navigation tools can help you remain on target.

Map and compass: A topographic map and a compass are required for conventional navigation. Before you go, practice reading maps and using a compass.

Use a GPS gadget or smartphone app for real-time tracking and navigation. Make sure your gadget is fully charged and keep a backup power source on hand in case you need it.

Track your route.

Keeping track of your journey allows you to avoid getting lost and retrace your steps if necessary.

Use waypoints or landmarks to track your journey. To aid navigation, keep an eye out for unusual features along the trail.

Consider utilizing a GPS tracking app to record your path. This can provide a digital record of your hike and aid in navigation if you need to retrace your travels.

Stay on the marked trails.

Following defined paths ensures that you stay on the proper route.

Trail markings: Pay attention to trail signs, blazes, and markings. These direct you along the prescribed route and help prevent deviations.

Trail maps: Carry a trail map and examine it on a frequent basis to validate your location and progress. To keep focused, compare the map to the real path.

Practice navigation skills.

Regular practice of navigation skills increases your confidence and efficacy.

Practice reading maps and using a compass. This will help you improve your navigating skills.

Prepare for tough paths by practicing navigation in familiar regions. This increases your abilities and confidence.

Use technology wisely.

Technology may be a great resource, but it must be used responsibly.

Battery Management: Charge electrical gadgets and carry a portable charger. Be aware of battery consumption and save power wherever feasible.

Prepare a backup navigation strategy in case technology fails. As a backup, always keep a physical map and compass on hand.

Solo hiking is a distinct and rewarding experience, but it demands careful planning, preparation, and alertness. Following these safety, path selection, and navigation suggestions can help you have a successful and fun solo hiking journey. Remember, the secret to successful solo hiking is to be prepared, vigilant, and follow your intuition. So lace up your boots, pack your stuff, and set off on your solo trip with confidence. Best wishes!

CHAPTER 14

HIKING FOR FITNESS
AND HEALTH

Hiking is more than simply a recreational activity; it's an effective approach to improve your physical fitness and overall health. Having spent years on the trails, I've witnessed personally how hiking can alter both body and mind. Whether you're an experienced hiker or a beginner, incorporating hiking into your workout program may be quite beneficial. In this chapter, I'll discuss the numerous physical health advantages of hiking, assist you in developing a tailored fitness plan, and demonstrate how to measure your progress and establish targets.

Advantages of Hiking for Physical Health

Hiking is a full-body activity with a variety of health advantages. Here's a closer look at how hiking the trails may improve your fitness and well-being.

Cardiovascular Health.

One of the most prominent advantages of hiking is its beneficial effect on cardiovascular health.

Hiking on different terrain improves heart health by increasing cardiovascular endurance. Regular hikes can help to control blood pressure and minimize the risk of heart disease.

Climbing hills and walking on uneven ground improves circulation and prevents varicose veins.

Weight Management.

Hiking is a great technique to control and keep a healthy weight.

Hiking can burn 400-700 calories per hour, depending on activity and terrain type. This makes it a great workout for weight loss and calorie control.

Regular hiking improves metabolism, allowing for more effective **calorie burn even at rest.**

Muscle Strength and Endurance.

Hiking utilizes several muscle groups, providing a complete exercise.

Hiking strengthens lower body muscles, including quadriceps, hamstrings, calves, and glutes, especially on steep stretches. This increases muscular strength and endurance in the lower body.

Maintaining core stability is crucial while navigating rough terrain. This strengthens the abdominal and lower back muscles.

Hiking with a backpack works up your upper body. Swinging your arms and using hiking poles can help build shoulder and arm strength.

Hiking can improve joint health if done appropriately.

Hiking is a low-impact workout that is better for your joints than jogging. The natural terrain helps to absorb impact and relieves stress on your knees and hips.

Hiking's diverse terrain promotes joint flexibility and range of motion. Walking on uneven surfaces causes your joints to adjust, which helps keep them healthy.

Mental Health and Well-being.

Hiking is beneficial to both your physical and emotional wellness.

Nature-based activities can relieve stress and anxiety. The peaceful setting of the outdoors offers a natural retreat from the stresses of everyday life.

Physical exercise releases endorphins, which can improve mood and reduce symptoms of depression. Hiking, with its stunning sights and fresh air, heightens this impact.

Developing a Fitness Plan

To get the most out of hiking for fitness, adopt a systematic plan. Here's how to create a fitness regimen that includes hiking efficiently.

Determine your current fitness level.

Before beginning, assess your current fitness level to personalize your regimen accordingly.

Physical Assessment: Evaluate your cardiovascular endurance, strength, flexibility, and hiking experience. This will allow you to establish realistic goals and select appropriate paths.

Consult a professional: If you have any health problems or issues, you should contact with a fitness expert or a healthcare practitioner before starting a new fitness program.

Set clear goals.

Determine what you hope to achieve with your hiking activity.

Fitness goals: Determine your fitness goals, such as increasing endurance, muscle gain, or weight loss. Specific goals will direct your training and keep you motivated.

Hiking goals: Set hiking goals, such as completing a set number of trails, traveling specified distances, or confronting more difficult terrain.

Plan your hiking schedule.

Make a plan to integrate hiking into your weekly routine.

Aim to hike 2-3 times each week. Adjust the frequency to match your fitness level and available time.

Start with shorter hikes and progressively increase time to improve fitness. A variety of easy, moderate, and difficult treks can assist improve general strength and endurance.

Incorporate cross-training.

Combine hiking with other types of exercise for a well-rounded fitness regimen.

Strength training activities such as squats, lunges, and core routines can help improve muscular strength. Strength training improves general fitness and helps to prevent injuries when trekking.

Cardio workouts: Increase your cardiovascular endurance and stamina by engaging in extra aerobic workouts such as cycling, swimming, or running.

Monitor and adjust your plan.

Regularly evaluate your progress and make improvements as required.

Track progress: Use a fitness app or diary to record distance, duration, and terrain throughout treks. Monitoring your progress allows you to remain on target and recognize improvements.

Adjust goals: As your fitness improves, modify your hiking objectives and difficulties. Continue to develop by gradually introducing more tougher paths or longer treks.

Tracking Progress and Goals

Tracking your progress and creating reasonable objectives are essential for remaining motivated and assessing your performance.

Use Fitness Apps and Tools.

Use technology to track your hiking activity and development.

GPS Tracking Apps: Use AllTrails, Strava, or Gaia GPS to track your route, mileage, and elevation gain. These applications give precise information about your treks, as well as assistance in setting and achieving objectives.

Wearable fitness monitors can track heart rate, calorie expenditure, and step count while hiking. This data allows you to assess your fitness level and track your progress.

Set SMART goals.

Use the SMART criteria to create effective and achievable objectives.

Define specific goals, such as trekking a certain distance or finishing a path.

Make your goals quantifiable. For example, strive to increase your trekking distance by two kilometers every month.

Set achievable objectives depending on your fitness level and available time. Gradually raise the difficulty as you advance.

Select goals that coincide with your fitness ambitions and hobbies. Make sure they are meaningful and motivational.

Create a time-bound plan to achieve your goals. This creates a sense of urgency and keeps you focused.

Reflect on Your Achievements.

Regularly evaluate your development and applaud your accomplishments.

Evaluate results. Evaluate how effectively you're accomplishing your objectives and whether your fitness is increasing. Evaluate your progress and make any necessary changes to your plan.

Celebrate milestones. Celebrate hitting milestones, such as finishing a difficult trek or setting a personal best. Recognizing your successes may increase motivation and confidence.

Adapt to Challenges

Be prepared to modify your strategy in response to obstacles or failures.

If you experience an accident or sickness, adapt your strategy accordingly. Concentrate on healing and adapt your training plan to meet your demands.

Inclement weather or trail conditions may affect hiking plans. Maintain your exercise program by incorporating alternate workouts or indoor hobbies.

Stay Motivated.

Maintaining motivation is critical to adhering to your exercise regimen.

Find Hiking Partners: Hiking with friends or a group may provide support and encouragement.

Add diversity to your hiking and workout program to keep things interesting. To keep yourself interested, explore new trails, various routines, and new difficulties.

Hiking is an excellent approach to improve your fitness and general health. You may maximize the benefits of hiking by recognizing its benefits, developing a disciplined fitness plan, and measuring your progress. Whether you want to improve your cardiovascular health, gain muscle, or simply enjoy the beautiful outdoors, hiking is a rewarding and effective way to get healthier. So, lace on your hiking boots, establish your objectives, and hit the trails—your path to fitness and well-being begins now. Happy trekking!

CHAPTER 15

ENVIRONMENTAL
CONSERVATION

As an experienced hiker, I've learned that our outdoor excursions come with responsibilities. The beauty and quiet of the outdoors are blessings that must be preserved for future generations. Understanding environmental protection is more than simply adhering to regulations; it also entails cultivating a true regard for nature. In this chapter, I'll go over the fundamentals of conservation, with an emphasis on Leave No Trace principles, local animal conservation, and environmental effect minimization. Following these rules will guarantee that our treks help to preserve our cherished landscapes.

Understanding the Leave No Trace Principles

The Leave No Trace (LNT) principles are critical for protecting the natural environment and keeping our trails immaculate. These principles are more than simply recommendations; they represent a commitment to ethical hiking and outdoor ethics.

Plan ahead and prepare.

With proper preparation, you may dramatically lessen your environmental effect.

Research your destination: Before you go trekking, investigate the region. Understand the local legislation, weather conditions, and any unique conservation requirements in the region.

Pack efficiently: Bring only what you need. Excessive equipment and supplies might cause wasteful waste. To limit waste, use reusable containers and minimize packing.

Travel and camp on durable surfaces.

Stick to well-established paths and campsites to minimize your effect.

Follow trails: Stay on recognized trails and avoid constructing new ones. This helps to reduce soil erosion and plant damage. To reduce trampling on plants, walk in the center of the route.

Use designated campsites: Camp only in authorized places. This protects sensitive habitats and inhibits the establishment of new, possibly harmful campsites.

Properly dispose of waste.

Proper trash disposal is critical to preserving a clean environment.

Pack it in and pack it out. Carry out all of your waste, including food leftovers, packaging, and personal hygiene products. Use trash bags to gather rubbish and leave nothing behind.

Follow waste disposal guidelines. Use the restrooms that are available. In places without facilities, dispose of human waste according to established norms, such as using a portable toilet or digging a kitty hole away from water sources.

Leave what you find.

Leave items exactly as you find them to preserve their inherent beauty.

Do not disturb nature: Avoid plucking plants, moving rocks, or disturbing wildlife. Leave natural features and artifacts intact for others to enjoy and to maintain ecological equilibrium.

Avoid cutting or marking natural surfaces, including trees and rocks. This protects the ecology and preserves the area's natural beauty.

Minimize the impact of the campfire

When campfires are not properly managed, they can have long-term environmental consequences.

If campfires are permitted, utilize designated fire rings or grills. This helps to keep the fire under control and protects the surrounding environment.

Burn wood completely. Burn the wood entirely to reduce residue and prevent leaving ashes behind. Instead of cooking over an open fire, consider utilizing a camp stove.

Respect wildlife.

Maintaining a respectful distance from animals is critical for their health and your safety.

Observe animals from a distance and avoid approaching or feeding them. Observing animals from a distance prevents habituation and reduces the likelihood of disrupting their normal behavior.

Ensure Food Security. Food should be stored correctly to prevent animals from obtaining it. To prevent attracting animals to your campground, use bear-proof containers or hang food out of reach.

Preserving Local Wildlife

Understanding and preserving the delicate balance of ecosystems is essential for local animal conservation. Every species contributes to the overall health of the environment.

Learn about local wildlife.

Understanding the local fauna allows you to cohabit with nature more peacefully.

Research animal species in your trekking area. Familiarize yourself with their routines, nutrition, and conservation issues.

Respect their space. Keep a safe distance from wildlife. Avoid surprising animals or approaching too closely, since this might create stress and disturb their usual habits.

Avoid disturbing habitats.

The preservation of animal habitats is critical to biodiversity conservation.

Stay on designated pathways to protect fragile ecosystems. This helps to safeguard plant species and nesting sites.

Be mindful of breeding seasons. Wildlife may be more susceptible at various times of year because they are reproducing or nesting.

Avoid disrupting these regions in order to safeguard young animals and their habitats.

Report wildlife sightings and issues.

If you experience problems with wildlife or see strange behavior, notify local authorities or park rangers.

Follow reporting procedures. Many parks and natural areas have established protocols for reporting wildlife observations or issues. This enables authorities to control wildlife populations and handle conservation concerns.

Contribute Information. Share your observations to support study and conservation. Providing correct information aids in the conservation and management of local species.

Support conservation efforts.

Participate in or support conservation projects.

Participate in volunteer programs. Many organizations provide volunteer opportunities in animal protection. Consider participating in projects that promote habitat restoration, animal monitoring, and educational outreach.

Donate to conservation groups. Donations to conservation groups support research, habitat protection, and wildlife management operations. Your assistance can have a big influence on conservation efforts.

Reducing your environmental impact

Minimizing your environmental effect entails being aware of how your activities influence the natural world. Adopting sustainable practices helps to preserve the environment.

Use environmentally friendly products.

Choosing eco-friendly items helps to lessen your environmental impact.

Use biodegradable soaps and toiletries. These goods degrade more easily and have a lower impact on natural water sources.

Use reusable containers, utensils, and water bottles. This cuts waste and decreases the demand for single-use plastics.

Water is a valuable resource that should be preserved.

Use water wisely for dishwashing and personal hygiene. Avoid putting soap directly into natural water sources, since it can damage aquatic life.

Respect water sources. Be careful near rivers, streams, and lakes. Do not contaminate these sources with garbage or chemicals.

Practice Responsible Photography Photography is a valuable tool for capturing memories, but it must be done carefully.

Avoid disturbing the environment: When photographing, avoid upsetting wildlife or harming flora and scenery. Use existing paths and vantage spots to get your photographs.

Leave No Trace with Photography Equipment: Make sure your photography equipment leaves no traces, such as rubbish or harm to natural elements.

Educate others

Sharing your understanding about environmental protection might motivate others to take responsibility.

Lead by example: Display strong conservation habits on your treks and urge others to do the same.

Share information: Use social media or community forums to raise awareness about environmental concerns and encourage appropriate hiking activities.

Support sustainable practices.

Support companies and organizations that promote sustainability.

Buy eco-friendly hiking gear and apparel from firms that prioritize sustainable materials and methods.

Support local conservation efforts. Contribute to or volunteer with local conservation groups dedicated to protecting natural places and animals.

Hiking provides an amazing chance to interact with nature; nevertheless, that luxury comes with the obligation to maintain and preserve the environment. We can preserve the beauty of our trails for future generations by learning and implementing Leave No Trace principles, protecting local species, and reducing our environmental effect. Every step we take should be cognizant of the natural world, and our actions should demonstrate a strong regard for the environment. So, as you put on your hiking boots and head out on your next expedition, remember to walk softly and leave merely footprints. Happy trekking, and happy conserving!

CHAPTER 16

PHOTOGRAPHY ON THE
TRAIL

There is something magical about capturing the beauty of a hike on film. Over the years, I've found that taking great photos on the trail is not just about snapping pictures—it's about preserving the essence of the adventure and sharing it with others. Whether you're a budding photographer or just want to capture your memories, knowing how to photograph nature effectively can elevate your hiking experience. Let's dive into how to capture scenic views, some tips for trail photography, and the best equipment to use while hiking.

Capturing Scenic Views

Every hike presents a new opportunity to capture stunning landscapes, but getting that perfect shot takes more than just pressing the shutter button. Here's how to make the most of your scenic photo opportunities:

Understanding Lighting.

Lighting can make or break a photograph, and natural light is your best friend on the trail.

Golden Hours: The best times for photography are during the golden hours—shortly after sunrise and before sunset. The soft, warm light during these times adds depth and warmth to your photos.

Avoid Harsh Midday Sun: The harsh light of midday can create strong shadows and wash out colors. If you're hiking during the middle of the day, look for shaded areas or overcast skies to diffuse the light.

Composition Techniques

Good composition is key to creating captivating photos.

The Rule of Thirds: Imagine your frame divided into nine equal parts by two equally spaced horizontal lines and two vertical lines.

Place your main subject along these lines or at their intersections to create a balanced composition.

Leading Lines: Use natural lines, like trails, rivers, or mountain ridges, to guide the viewer's eye into the photo. This can create a sense of depth and perspective.

Framing: Frame your subject with natural elements, like trees or rocks, to draw attention to it and add context to the scene.

Capturing Details

While wide-angle images are fantastic for capturing sweeping landscapes, close-ups may highlight the exquisite beauty of nature.

Focus on Details: Look for intriguing textures, patterns, or colors in plants, rocks, or fauna. These close-up photographs may compliment your bigger landscape photos and highlight the finer details of the surroundings.

Macro Photography: If you have a macro lens or setting, use it to take detailed photos of flowers, insects, or other natural features that may otherwise go missed.

Experiment with Angles

Changing your perspective may lead to interesting and fascinating images.

High and Low Angles: Try shooting from different heights. A low perspective can make flowers or little plants look bigger, while a high angle might provide a broader picture of the area.

Get Creative: Experiment with unconventional angles and viewpoints. Sometimes the most striking photos come from seeing the scene from a new perspective.

Tips for Trail Photography

Taking amazing images while hiking includes more than simply knowing what to shoot—it's also about how you shoot. Here are some practical strategies to boost your trail photography:

Carry your camera thoughtfully.

Balancing convenience with security is critical.

Use a lightweight camera: If you don't want to carry a bulky DSLR, try a tiny mirrorless camera or a high-quality smartphone with a decent camera. They are more portable while yet producing outstanding results.

Protect Your Gear: When not in use, store your camera in a waterproof case or plastic bag to protect it from unexpected weather. This will help keep it safe from rain, dust, and moisture.

Master your camera settings.

Understanding your camera's settings may greatly improve your images.

Use manual or semi-manual settings to adjust exposure: Adjust the aperture, shutter speed, and ISO to acquire the optimal exposure for your conditions.

Focus and Depth of Field: Use a shallow depth of field (wide aperture) for close-up images to blur the backdrop and accent your subject. A deep depth of field (narrow aperture) helps to keep everything in focus while shooting landscapes.

Be prepared for the moment.

Nature is full of transient moments that are often overlooked.

Make sure your camera is conveniently accessible. A camera strap or a chest-mounted camera bag might help you swiftly retrieve your equipment when you see something fascinating.

Be Patient: Sometimes the finest photos need patience. Before shooting a photograph, wait for the correct light, the perfect time, or the optimal viewpoint.

Respect the environment.

While capturing nature's beauty, it is also crucial to respect it.

Minimize disturbance to animals and natural ecosystems. Avoid going too near to animals or trampling on flora to obtain a good image.

Use Leave No Trace guidelines to minimize environmental effect when photographing. Remove any rubbish and avoid harming the natural environment.

Share your photos thoughtfully.

Once you've taken those incredible photos, share them in a way that preserves the environment and encourages safe hiking.

When publishing images on social media, include conservation and nature-related information. Encourage people to enjoy the outdoors responsibly.

When sharing images from a trail or park, make sure you credit the location and follow any requirements. This can help people appreciate and respect the surroundings.

Recommended Hiking Equipment

Choosing the appropriate equipment may significantly improve your trail photography experience. Here's a list of the essential tools and accessories:

Camera Options.

Different types of cameras have distinct benefits.

Smartphone: High-quality cameras and built-in editing capabilities are common features on modern smartphones. They're lightweight and easy to transport, making them ideal for casual hikers.

Compact cameras are smaller, lighter, and produce higher image quality than smartphones. They're an excellent alternative if you want something more complex without hauling a lot of baggage.

Mirrorless cameras offer outstanding image quality and versatility while remaining small. They include interchangeable lenses and advanced functionality while being relatively lightweight.

Lenses.

The lens you choose might have an impact on how versatile your photography is.

Wide-angle lenses are ideal for photographing expansive vistas and sceneries. They allow you to fit more into the frame and provide a dramatic impression.

Zoom lenses are useful for animals and distant objects. A zoom lens allows you to come closer to the action without really moving.

Macro lenses are ideal for capturing close-up images of minute things in nature. They allow you to capture detailed textures and patterns.

Accessories

The appropriate accessories might improve your photographic experience.

Use a lightweight tripod to support your camera and capture better shots, especially in low-light or long exposures.

Bring additional batteries and memory cards to avoid running out of power or storage during your journey.

Lens cleaning kit: Dust and wetness can damage your photographs. A lens cleaning kit keeps your camera lens clean and free of smudges.

Editing tools

Post-processing may improve your images, but you must utilize it to supplement your original shots.

Mobile apps like Snapseed and Adobe Lightroom Mobile provide advanced editing tools on the fly. They let you change exposure, contrast, and color balance directly from your phone.

Desktop software, such as Adobe Lightroom or Photoshop, offers advanced editing tools to enhance and refine photographs.

Photography on the trail is about more than simply taking beautiful pictures; it's about recording the adventure and sharing the beauties of nature with others. Understanding how to capture breathtaking vistas, implementing practical photography strategies, and utilizing the correct equipment will help you improve your hiking experiences and create memorable memories. So, the next time you lace up your boots and hit the trail, carry your camera and let the beauty of nature inspire your creativity. Happy photography, and here's to capturing the soul of each journey!

CHAPTER 17

HIKING AND CAMPING

Combining hiking with camping elevates the trip to a new level. There's something very fulfilling about capping off a day on the path with a night beneath the stars, surrounded by nature's tranquility. For me, it's a way to lengthen the experience by enjoying both the route and the goal. If you're thinking about adding camping to your hiking itinerary, let's look at how to effortlessly combine the two activities, identify the finest campgrounds near Spokane trails, and prepare for an unforgettable outdoor adventure.

Combining Hiking and Camping

Hiking and camping are a terrific opportunity to totally immerse yourself in the great outdoors. Here's how to get the most out of this combination adventure:

Plan Your Itinerary.

When organizing a hiking and camping vacation, it is critical to devise a well-planned itinerary that balances trekking and camping.

Distance and difficulty: Choose a trek that is appropriate for your fitness level and interests, taking in mind the distance to the campground. Choose paths that provide lovely camping areas or authorized campsites.

Plan your journey so you arrive at your campsite with enough daylight to set up and settle in before dusk. Arrive early enough to appreciate the scenery and perhaps explore a little more.

Selecting a Campsite

Selecting the proper location may have a significant influence on your camping experience.

Select campsites with scenic views or close to water sources. Being near a lake or river might improve the experience and give a relaxing background sound for sleep.

For a good night's sleep, put up your tent in a flat and well-drained area. Avoid areas that accumulate water or are too near to the route or cliff edge.

Safety: Locate your campsite away from potential threats including falling boulders, avalanche tracks, and unstable terrain. Also, look for wildlife activity and pick a location that minimizes confrontations with animals.

Packing smartly

Packing efficiently for a hiking and camping vacation entails bringing everything you require without overburdening yourself.

Hiking gear: Bring necessities such as a map, compass, first-aid kit, and enough food and drink for the trek. For longer travels, consider bringing a hydration system or a water filter.

Use lightweight, compact camping gear to lighten your burden. A tent, sleeping bag, sleeping pad, and camping stove or cooking equipment are all essential.

Setting up camp.

Once you arrive at your campground, setting up properly will make your stay more comfortable.

Follow the manufacturer's directions to set up your tent. Before settling in, ensure that it is adequately staked down and that there are no leaks or damage.

Keep your things organized and accessible. Food and other goods that may attract wildlife should be stored in a tent vestibule or bear-proof container.

Campfire safety: If you want to have a campfire, be sure it's authorized and follow any local rules. Build it in a specified fire ring, and keep it small. Never leave a fire unattended, and extinguish it completely before retiring to bed.

Top Campsites Near Spokane Trails

Spokane has a variety of trails that blend perfectly with good camping possibilities. Here are some of the best campgrounds along major Spokane trails:

Riverside State Park is conveniently located near downtown Spokane and offers excellent hiking and camping opportunities.

Highlights of the park's campgrounds: The Bowl and Pitcher Campground gives easy access to trails and stunning views of the Spokane River.

The park's popular trails include the Spokane River Centennial Trail and the Iller Creek Conservation Area, which provide stunning views and diverse terrain.

Mount Spokane State Park.

Mount Spokane State Park is located northeast of Spokane and offers excellent hiking and camping opportunities.

The park has many campsites, including Mount Spokane Campground, which is close to trailheads.

Popular Trails: The Mount Spokane Trail and CCC Trail provide diverse hiking experiences with stunning views of the surrounding mountains.

Colville National Forest, located an hour north of Spokane, offers a more isolated camping experience.

Campsite Highlights: The forest offers multiple campgrounds and dispersed camping options. The Sullivan Lake Campground is a popular choice due to its gorgeous lakefront setting.

Popular paths include the Sullivan Lake Trail and the Salmo-Priest Wilderness Area, which offer breathtaking natural beauty and different ecosystems.

Palouse Falls State Park

Located 1.5 hours southwest of Spokane, Palouse Falls State Park is known for its impressive waterfall.

The park provides a small campground with views of the falls. It's an ideal location for anyone wishing to enjoy both the climb and the breathtaking waterfall.

Popular Trails: The Palouse Falls Trail offers scenic views of the falls and surrounding environment, making it an ideal short stroll before or after camping.

Steptoe Butte State Park :is located about an hour south of Spokane and offers panoramic views of the Palouse area.

Campsite highlights: While the park does not have constructed campgrounds, there are some dispersed camping opportunities nearby. The surrounding town of Colfax provides services and prospective camping areas.

Popular trails include the Steptoe Butte Trail, which offers stunning vistas of the Palouse environment.

Essential Camping Gear

Having the correct gear is essential for comfort and safety when hiking and camping. Here's a full list of important camping equipment to bring along.

Tent: Choose the appropriate size and kind for your group's needs. Solo hikers choose a lightweight one-person tent, however families or parties may require larger tents with greater space and conveniences.

Choose a tent with strong weather protection, such as a rainfly and waterproof floor. Ventilation is also vital to avoid dampness within.

Sleeping Bag

Temperature Rating: Select a sleeping bag with a temperature rating adequate for the conditions you expect. For colder conditions, choose a bag with a lower temperature rating or add a sleeping bag liner for added warmth.

Insulation type: Select between down and synthetic insulation. Down is lighter and more compressible, but it loses insulation when wet, whereas synthetic insulation works better in damp situations.

Sleeping Pad

Provides comfort and insulation from the ground. Inflatable pads provide more comfort and portability, whilst foam pads are more durable and cost-effective.

Cooking Equipment

A lightweight camping stove or portable burner is required for cooking. Canister stoves are suitable for most expeditions, although liquid-fuel stoves may be required for longer or more distant excursions.

Bring lightweight cookware and utensils for your meals. Do not forget to bring a portable sink or a small container for washing dishes.

Food and Water

Meal planning Prepare your meals ahead of time and carry non-perishable, easy-to-cook goods. Dehydrated meals, trail mix, and energy snacks are ideal for convenience and weight loss.

Bring a water filter or purification tablets for hiking in areas with unreliable water supplies. Bring enough water containers to remain hydrated throughout your journey.

Illumination

A headlamp or lantern is useful for hands-free illumination and navigating about the campground at night. A camping lantern offers ambient lighting for cooking and resting.

Clothing and Personal Items.

Pack layers for changing temperatures. Use moisture-wicking base layers, insulating layers, and a waterproof shell.

When camping in rural areas, bring personal hygiene products such as a toothbrush, biodegradable soap, and a tiny shovel for digging a kitty hole. 8. Safety and First Aid.

First aid kit: A well-stocked first aid kit should include essentials such as bandages, antiseptics, pain medicines, and any personal prescriptions.

Emergency items: Bring a multi-tool, fire starter, and emergency whistle. Even if you have a GPS gadget, it is always a good idea to have a map and compass.

Combining hiking with camping may be a really enjoyable experience, providing a deeper connection to nature and more opportunities to explore. You may assure a safe, pleasant, and memorable vacation by carefully planning your trip, selecting appropriate campsites, and bringing necessary items. Whether you're setting up camp beside a tranquil lake, among towering pines, or on a craggy summit, the combination of hiking and camping guarantees an engaging experience that takes you closer to the heart of the nature. Enjoy your journeys, and may your evenings beneath the stars be as breathtaking as the routes you travel!

CHAPTER 18

OVERCOMING HIKING CHALLENGES

Hiking, although wonderfully gratifying, is not without its hardships. From altitude sickness and blisters to staying motivated on long hikes, every hiker experiences challenges at some time. Drawing on my years of hiking experience, I want to provide thoughts and tactics for overcoming these typical problems, so you're ready for anything the path throws at you.

Dealing with altitude sickness

Altitude sickness is a major issue for individuals attempting high-altitude excursions. As you get over 8,000 feet (2,400 meters), the air pressure lowers and there is less oxygen available. This decline might cause symptoms such as headaches, dizziness, nausea, and exhaustion. Here's how to manage and reduce altitude sickness:

Gradual ascent.

The most effective strategy to avoid altitude sickness is to ascend gently. Allow your body to adapt by taking rest days at intermediate levels. If your hike requires a large altitude gain, prepare for incremental elevation gains rather than pressing straight to high heights.

Hydration & Nutrition

Staying hydrated is essential at high elevations. Dehydration worsens altitude sickness symptoms, so drink lots of water. A balanced, carbohydrate-rich diet can also assist. Carbohydrates are easy to digest and give rapid energy, which is useful when your oxygen levels drop.

Recognize symptoms. Early

Be wary of altitude sickness symptoms, which can vary from minor headaches to more serious diseases such as high-altitude pulmonary edema (HAPE) or high-altitude cerebral edema (HACE). Mild symptoms like as headaches and nausea can typically be treated with rest, fluids, and drugs such as acetazolamide (Diamox), which help with acclimatization.

Immediate action

If symptoms increase or do not improve, descend to a lower altitude. This is the most effective therapy for altitude sickness. While descending may appear to be a setback, it is really vital for your safety and well-being.

Medical attention.

Seek medical assistance right once if you have severe symptoms or if they continue despite your efforts to improve. To handle major altitude-related disorders, it is preferable to take precautions and seek expert assistance.

Treating Blisters and Other Common Injuries

Blisters and other minor ailments may rapidly transform a pleasurable trip into an unpleasant experience. Fortunately, with the correct tactics and planning, you can handle and avoid these issues:

Proper footwear and socks.

The core of blister prevention is to wear well-fitting hiking boots and moisture-wicking socks. Boots should be broken in before going on a lengthy trip to avoid friction that might cause blisters. Choose socks composed of synthetic fibers or merino wool, which drain moisture away from the skin and minimize friction.

Blister Prevention.

Consider utilizing blister prevention tools like blister pads, tape, or specific blister prevention socks. Apply these items on areas prone to friction, such as heels and toes, before hitting the trails. If you sense a hot area, apply tape or other protective materials right away.

Treating Blisters.

If you acquire a blister, careful treatment is required to avoid infection and additional suffering. Here's how to handle it:

If the blister has popped, carefully clean the area with soap and water. Apply an antibiotic ointment to avoid infection.

To protect the blister, cover it with a sterile bandage or blister pad. Make sure the covering isn't too tight and allows some ventilation into the space.

To reduce infection risk, avoid puncturing or bursting blisters. If a blister bursts, clean and cover it as directed.

Dealing With Other Injuries

In addition to blisters, hikers also sustain minor injuries such as sprains, strains, and cuts. Here's a brief guide for handling these injuries:

To manage sprains and strains, use the R.I.C.E. method (rest, ice, compression, and elevation). Apply ice to the wounded region, cover it in an elastic bandage, and elevate it to minimize swelling.

For cuts and scrapes, clean wounds with water and mild soap. Apply antibacterial ointment and wrap with a sterile bandage. Inspect the injury for symptoms of infection.

Emergency First Aid bag A well-stocked first aid bag is crucial for addressing accidents on the trail. Include supplies such as sticky bandages, antibacterial wipes, blister treatment, and any personal prescriptions. Knowing how to utilize these products successfully can make a big difference in how quickly you can treat an injury.

Strategies to Stay Motivated

Staying motivated on lengthy walks on hard paths may be just as difficult as the physical effort itself. Here are some ways for keeping your motivation and spirits up:

Set clear goals.

Set clear hiking goals before you go. Whether it's achieving a specific perspective, covering a certain distance, or simply spending time in nature, having defined goals may help you stay focused and motivated.

Break it down.

Breaking up long walks into smaller, more manageable chunks might make them appear less overwhelming. Instead of worrying about the entire trek, concentrate on completing one milestone at a time, such as a picturesque area or a checkpoint. Celebrate every victory along the road.

Find enjoyment in the journey

Enjoy the voyage and take time to admire your surroundings. Pause to take in the scenery, listen to the sounds of nature, and cherish moments of isolation or fellowship with other hikers. When motivation is low, taking pleasure in the trip might give a lift.

Stay Positive

Maintain a good attitude, even when things are rough. Remind yourself why you began the hike in the first place, and concentrate on the positive elements of the experience. Encouragement from friends, inspiring slogans, or simply recalling oneself of previous hiking accomplishments may all help raise your morale.

Use Distraction Techniques.

Distraction may sometimes be an effective motivator. Listen to music, an audiobook, or a podcast while hiking to distract yourself from exhaustion or pain. Conversation with trekking buddies can also help pass the time and lift your emotions.

Prepare for Challenges

Anticipate foreseeable obstacles and plan accordingly. Understand that you may encounter difficult areas, and having a strategy in place will help you cope with these situations when they happen. Visualization tactics, such as envisioning yourself at the top or finishing the path, can also help you stay focused.

Reflect on your accomplishments

After finishing a trek, take some time to reflect on your accomplishments. Consider writing, photographing, or sharing your adventure with others. Reflecting on your accomplishments might help you stay motivated for future hikes.

Hiking obstacles, both physical and emotional, are part of the trip. By being prepared for altitude sickness, controlling blisters and injuries, and utilizing motivational tactics, you may overcome these challenges with confidence and continue to enjoy the great experiences that hiking provides. Remember that each struggle faced is a step toward becoming a stronger, more resilient hiker. Embrace the adventure, learn from each experience, and let the beauty of the trails motivate you to keep going. Happy trekking!

CHAPTER 19

HISTORICAL AND CULTURAL ASPECTS OF THE SPOKANE TRAILS

As an experienced hiker who has spent countless hours exploring the trails surrounding Spokane, I have learned to appreciate not just the natural beauty, but also the rich historical and cultural tapestry that these routes weave. Hiking in Spokane provides more than just physical activity and magnificent vistas; it allows you to connect with the area's history and learn about the cultures that have created the region. In this chapter, I'll take you on a tour through the historical significance of local trails, highlighting cultural locations and landmarks while also delving into the indigenous history and viewpoints that are woven into the fabric of these pathways.

The Historical Significance of Local Trails

The trails surrounding Spokane are more than just roads through the forest; they are historical corridors that convey the tale of millennia of human-environmental interactions. Let's look at some of the historical elements that give these routes their distinct character.

The Spokane River Trail.

The Spokane River Trail is more than just a gorgeous route; it's a living history book. This pathway follows the Spokane River from Spokane Falls to Lake Spokane, tracing the paths used by early explorers and settlers. The Spokane River was an important transportation route for fur traders and adventurers in the nineteenth century. Walking down this route, one can almost envision the hustle and bustle of a bygone era when steamboats and canoes were the principal modes of transportation.

The Centennial Trail.

This trail, which runs from Spokane to the Idaho border, is not only a popular hiking route, but it also represents an important piece of area history. Established to mark Spokane's centennial in 1991, the route has since become a community staple, connecting several parks and natural areas. As you stroll, you'll see historical markers and interpretive signage that explain Spokane's development and the trail's significance in linking neighborhoods.

Riverside State Park.

Riverside State Park has full with historical significance. This park, established in the early twentieth century, has long served as a hub for outdoor activity in Spokane. The trails here provide views into the history of the Civilian Conservation Corps (CCC) during the Great Depression, since CCC workers built many of the park's facilities and trails. Hiking around Riverside State Park allows you to appreciate both the natural beauty and the historical endeavors that formed it.

Beacon Hill

Beacon Hill is renowned for its panoramic views and historical significance. During World War II, it was utilized for military training exercises, and the paths still contain vestiges of former military structures. Beacon Hill also had a role in the area's early forestry history, with historic logging roads being part of the hiking trail system.

The Spokane Arboretum

The Spokane Arboretum paths provide a unique historical experience by focusing on plant history. The arboretum was developed to display the region's unique plant life and has served as a valuable research and educational facility. Hiking here provides an opportunity to learn about initiatives to preserve and study native plant species, as well as their historical significance in the local ecology.

Cultural sites and landmarks

In addition to their historical significance, many of Spokane's paths are linked to cultural institutions and landmarks. These sites provide a glimpse into the region's cultural heritage and a better knowledge of its history.

Spokane Falls.

Spokane Falls, accessible via the Riverfront Park trail system, is both a spectacular natural feature and a cultural icon. The original Spokane people viewed the falls as a holy spot. For years, the falls have served as a focal point for neighborhood festivals and cultural activities, cementing its place in Spokane's history.

Manito Park

with its paths, gardens, and historic elements, exemplifies Spokane's dedication to public spaces and cultural enrichment. The park's Duncan Garden and Japanese Garden represent the cultural influences that have influenced the city. These gardens provide a calm respite and an opportunity to reflect on the ethnic variety that contributes to Spokane's distinct character.

The Spokane County Historical Museum.

The Spokane County Historical Museum, while not a trail, is an invaluable resource for anybody interested in Spokane's cultural and historical backdrop. The museum, located on some prominent trails, has displays and information that can help you comprehend the areas you're hiking through. It's worth a stop before or after your climb to gain a better sense of the region's cultural landscape.

The Hillyard District

The Hillyard District, accessible by local paths, is a historic area with origins in the early twentieth century. It was once a thriving railroad center and is now a great place to explore on foot. Walking around Hillyard provides insight into Spokane's history and varied community.

The WSU Spokane campus

The Washington State University Spokane campus, which is located near various trails, has historical and cultural sites. The site contains the Spokane Teaching Health Clinic and the Riverpoint site, both of which contribute to the city's overall educational and cultural scene. Exploring the environment around campus might offer perspective to your hiking trip.

Indigenous History and Perspectives

The indigenous peoples of the Spokane region have a deep and enduring connection to their land. Understanding their histories and opinions enriches your trekking experience. Here's a closer look at indigenous history and how it connects to Spokane's trails.

The Spokane Tribe.

The Spokane Tribe, after which the city is named, has inhabited in the area for thousands of years. Their traditional domains encompass the area surrounding the Spokane River and its tributaries. The paths you travel frequently pass through areas that have been important to the tribe's culture and subsistence. The Spokane people have a strong spiritual connection to the land, and many of the routes are historically significant to them.

Sacred sites and traditional lands.

The Spokane Tribe considers some spots along Spokane's pathways holy. For example, Spokane Falls is regarded as a spiritual location. The tribe's oral traditions and cultural activities are inextricably linked to these natural aspects. When trekking in these places, it's critical to respect their cultural value and recognize that you're passing through territories that have great meaning for the indigenous people.

Cultural Preservation Efforts.

The Spokane Tribe and other indigenous communities are actively interested in preserving and sharing their traditional history. Many of the trails and parks you visit are managed collaboratively by local governments and tribal organizations to ensure that their cultural and historical value is honored and preserved. Participating in these initiatives, whether through educational programs or cultural events, contributes to the continuous preservation of indigenous traditions.

Learning from Indigenous Perspectives.

Participating in guided tours or educational programs given by tribal groups can help you develop a better understanding of indigenous viewpoints. These programs frequently use storytelling, traditional customs, and cultural insights to improve your hiking experience. They provide the chance to learn directly from the indigenous population and obtain a better grasp of the region's cultural history.

Observing Cultural Protocols

When trekking in places of indigenous significance, it is essential to respect cultural customs. This involves adhering to any access limitations at specific places, avoiding damaging holy locations, and being aware of the land's cultural values. By treating your climb with respect and understanding, you help to preserve indigenous history while also fostering beneficial interactions between hikers and local people.

Exploring Spokane's trails is more than simply a physical excursion; it allows you to connect with the region's rich historical and cultural heritage. From comprehending the historical importance of the trails to recognizing cultural monuments to honoring indigenous history, each trek provides a chance to interact with the land's deeper tales.

As you lace up your hiking boots and head out onto the trails, take a time to consider the history beneath your feet and the cultural value of the landscapes around you. Every step you take is part of a broader narrative that spans generations, and realizing this enriches your hiking experience while also contributing to the continued awareness and preservation of Spokane's unique legacy.

Happy trekking, and may your time in Spokane be filled with exploration, respect, and a stronger connection to the land and its tales.

CHAPTER 20

GEOCACHING AND OUTDOOR GAMES

As a frequent hiker and outdoor enthusiast, I've discovered that adding a sense of fun and humor to a trek may make it even more memorable. One of my favorite methods to accomplish this is through geocaching and outdoor activities. If you've never had either, you're in for a treat. Both activities may turn a simple stroll into a thrilling treasure hunt or a fun-filled day of games. In this chapter, I'll go over the basics of geocaching, highlight several popular geocaching routes in Spokane, and recommend a few outdoor activities to make your excursions even more enjoyable.

Introduction to Geocaching

Let's begin with geocaching, which is essentially a high-tech treasure hunt involving GPS. The idea is simple: users conceal containers, or "caches," at certain coordinates and then broadcast those coordinates online. Your aim is to uncover these hidden caches using a GPS gadget or smartphone.

How Geocaching Works

Geocaching starts with discovering a geocache site online. Geocaching.com, for example, provides coordinates and clues to caches buried all around the world. You use your GPS or a geocaching app to find the site, where you'll look for a concealed container containing a logbook and occasionally tiny trinkets or toys to trade. The plan is to sign the logbook to confirm you discovered the cache and leave a little item of equal or better value in return for any treasure you find.

Types of Geocaches

There are numerous sorts of geocaches you might encounter:

Traditional caches: These are the basic kind of geocaches. The coordinates mentioned are where you can find the cache.

Multi-Caches: These need numerous stages, with each cache leading to the next set of coordinates.

Mystery or Puzzle Caches: Solve a puzzle to get the final coordinates.

Letterbox Hybrid is a combination of geocaching and letterboxing, needing both GPS and clues.

Why Geocaching Is Ideal for Hikers

Geocaching brings fun and curiosity to your hikes. It's more than just following a trail; it's about leveraging clues and technology to find hidden gems. Furthermore, it can bring you to new paths and regions you would not have discovered otherwise. It's an excellent method to interact with the outdoors while keeping both children and adults amused.

Popular Geocaching Trails in Spokane

Spokane has a thriving geocaching community, with several routes and locations to discover hidden caches. Here are some popular geocaching destinations in and near Spokane:

Riverfront Park.

Riverfront Park is a major site in Spokane and a popular geocaching destination. The park's large network of paths, along with its historical and scenic aspects, make it ideal for geocaching. Look for caches at sites such as Spokane Falls and the park's several bridges.

Riverside State Park.

Riverside State Park's huge breadth and diversified topography provide several geocaching chances. Trails here go through woodlands, beside rivers, and past historical monuments. You could locate caches concealed in interesting places, such as near ancient CCC facilities or picturesque overlooks.

Manito Park

Manito Park, with its stunning gardens and paths, is another excellent geocaching location. The park's several themed gardens and arboretum are ideal locations for cache installation. As you tour this popular park, take in the natural beauty and hidden discoveries.

Beacon Hill

Beacon Hill is famed for its panoramic vistas and rocky terrain, making it an ideal location for geocaching. The route network here is a combination of difficult walks and gorgeous sites, with caches frequently buried in unique and surprising locations.

Mount Spokane State Park

Mount Spokane State Park offers a more adventurous geocaching experience. The park's vast trails and diverse topography provide a variety of caches, from simple discoveries to more difficult hunts. The elevation fluctuations and different settings give another dimension of excitement to your geocaching trip.

Spokane Valley's Centennial Trail

This path, which runs from Spokane to the Idaho border, is popular for its length and diversity. There are various geocaches buried along the walk, including those in parks, along the river, and near attractive vistas. It's an excellent way to combine a lengthy journey with the excitement of treasure seeking.

Palouse-to-Cascades Trail

The Palouse to Cascades Trail, located just west of Spokane, combines rail-trail with picturesque hiking activities. With its lengthy lengths and historical monuments, you're sure to find some intriguing geocaches along the way.

Little Spokane River Natural Area.

The Little Spokane River Natural Area boasts beautiful woodlands and calm river vistas. It's a lovely hiking destination with plenty of well-hidden geocaches in a natural setting.

Spokane's South Hill

The South Hill region, with its network of paths and parks, contains a number of hidden geocaches. The urban and semi-rural combination creates a diversified geocaching experience, with caches buried in parks, trails, and near local monuments.

Liberty Lake Regional Park.

Liberty Lake Regional Park is a little further away but has an excellent variety of trails and geocaches. The park's diverse environment and enormous size make it an ideal spot for a day of hiking and treasure seeking.

Fun Outdoor Games & Activities

Geocaching isn't the only option to add some excitement to your journey. There are several additional outdoor sports and activities that might complement your trekking experience. Here are some of my favorites:

Scavenger Hunt.

A scavenger hunt is a great way to make your trek more interesting. Make a list of objects to look for along the route, such as certain types of leaves, pebbles, or wildlife, and compete to see who can discover the most of them. It's an excellent technique to promote observation and involvement with the environment.

Trail Bingo adds a competitive element to hiking: Create bingo cards with trail-related elements like "squirrel sighting," "waterfall," and "wildflower." Mark off the objects you come across while hiking. The first player to finish a row or the whole card wins!

Nature Photo Contest

Bring a camera or use your smartphone to document the beauty of your hike. Create a photography contest with categories such as "best landscape shot" and "most interesting wildlife photo." Share your images with friends and family to discover who captured the finest moments.

Wildlife Tracking.

Wildlife tracking is an enjoyable and educational pastime. Look for animal footprints, scats, and other wildlife indications while hiking. Use field guides or applications to identify the creatures that may have left the footprints. It's an excellent opportunity to learn about the local wildlife and improve your trekking experience.

Geocaching Relay.

If you're hiking with a group, make geocaching a relay race. Divide into teams and see who can discover the most caches in the allotted period of time. It's a great way to include some friendly competition and collaboration into your trek.

Storytelling Circle.

Find a lovely area to rest and assemble your company for a storytelling circle. Share experiences from previous walks, make up adventure stories, or recite local folklore. It's an excellent way to connect and make lifelong memories.

Orienteering Challenge.

Combine your hike with an orienteering challenge. To travel along the path, use a compass and a map. Set some checkpoints and see who can locate them the quickest. It's a terrific method to improve your navigation abilities while also making your journey more enjoyable.

Nature Art Use natural resources from the route, such as leaves, rocks, and sticks, to make art. Arrange them into patterns or designs, then photograph your creations. It's a unique approach to interact with the environment without leaving no trace.

Birdwatching

Bring a bird guide or app to identify bird species throughout your trek. Make a list of birds to watch and see how many you can find. Birdwatching provides a new depth to your trip and allows you to connect with the local bird population.

Fitness challenges.

Incorporate fitness challenges into your trek, such as running intervals or strength workouts in picturesque locations. Set personal objectives or compete with friends to see who can finish the tasks fastest. It's an excellent method to mix workout with outdoor activities.

Geocaching and outdoor activities may elevate your trekking experience. Whether you're looking for hidden riches or playing fascinating games along the path, these activities add to the thrill and enjoyment of your trip. Spokane's trails provide an ideal backdrop for both, with several geocaching locations and chances for outdoor play.

So, the next time you lace up your hiking boots, try including a geocaching hunt or a fun game into your itinerary. It's an excellent way to maximize your time outside, connect with nature, and produce memorable memories. Happy trekking, and may your routes be full of excitement and delight!

CHAPTER 21

NIGHT HIKE AND STARGAZING

If you've ever pondered extending your hiking trips into the night, you're in for an extraordinary experience. Night hiking and stargazing provide a fresh viewpoint on the trails, offering views and feelings that you would not meet during the day. The tranquility of a night trek, paired with the immensity of the night sky, may transform an average excursion into a magnificent adventure. In this chapter, I'll walk you through the fundamentals of night hiking and stargazing, including safety precautions, the finest paths for stargazing, and the equipment you'll need to make the most of your evening experience.

Safety Guidelines for Night Hiking

Night hiking may be thrilling, but it takes careful planning to ensure a safe and fun experience. Here are some important safety guidelines to keep in mind.

Know Your Trail.

Before you go, properly investigate the path you intend to climb. Familiarize yourself with the landscape, identifying any risks and problematic locations. If you're new to night hiking, start on a path you've already trekked during the day. This familiarity will allow you to maneuver more comfortably in the darkness.

Plan ahead.

Check out the weather prediction for the night before your hike. Weather conditions might change quickly, so you should be prepared for any potential problems. If thunderstorms or severe rain are anticipated, postpone your hike. Also, plan your route and have a clear turnaround time to prevent being out in the dark for too long.

Bring a reliable headlamp or flashlight.

A dependable light source is essential for night hikes. Headlamps are especially handy since they free up your hands, making it easier to maneuver and deal with obstructions. Make sure your headlamp has a red light setting to protect your night vision. Carry additional batteries or a backup flashlight in case of an emergency.

Wear reflective gear.

Wear fluorescent clothes or gear to increase your visibility to others, particularly if you're hiking in regions where other people may be present. This is especially vital if you're near roadways or trailheads, where visibility is critical.

Stay on the marked trails.

Stick to recognized trails and avoid cutting across unfamiliar terrain. In the dark, it's easy to lose your way or accidentally go off-trail, which may lead to accidents or being lost. Marked trails are often safer and more predictable.

Move at a comfortable pace.

Navigating in the dark might be difficult, so take your time and proceed at a speed that seems natural. Keep your footing and be aware of potential tripping risks such as roots or pebbles. Allow yourself to pause periodically to change your lighting and assess your surroundings.

Hike in a group.

If feasible, go hiking in a group or at least one other person. There is safety in numbers, and having someone beside you can provide reassurance. Additionally, sharing the experience may be a lot of fun.

Carry a map and compass.

Even if you're familiar with the path, having a map and compass is a smart idea. GPS gadgets sometimes fail, so having classic navigation tools can help you stay on track if necessary. Before you go hiking, be sure you know how to utilize them.

Inform someone about your plans.

Tell a friend or family member about your trekking plans, including your projected return time. This way, if something goes wrong, they may notify authorities and offer important information about your whereabouts.

Prepare for Wildlife Encounters.

Wildlife may be more active at night, so be cautious of your surroundings. Make sounds while hiking to warn animals to your presence, but avoid approaching or frightening wildlife.

Best Trails for Stargazing

Stargazing while hiking might be one of the most relaxing and uplifting experiences you can have. The lack of light pollution and the tranquility of the night make for an ideal backdrop to stare at the stars. Here are some of the greatest routes in and near Spokane that combine hiking with stargazing:

Mount Spokane.

Mount Spokane provides some of the greatest stargazing possibilities in the region owing to its elevation and limited light pollution. The summit's wide vistas create a spectacular canvas for watching the night sky. The trek to the peak might be difficult, so be prepared and allow plenty of time to admire the stars once you arrive.

Riverside State Park.

Riverside State Park is another great spot for astronomy. The park's expansive size and varied terrain provide several observation spots. The region surrounding the Spokane River may be quite peaceful and ideal for a night beneath the stars.

Palouse-to-Cascades Trail

This route covers a large region with low light pollution. Several portions of the path provide unimpeded views of the night sky. For the finest stargazing experience, choose a location that is remote from any surrounding towns or cities.

Liberty Lake Regional Park.

Liberty Lake Regional Park is a little further away, but it's definitely worth the trek. The park's large open expanses and distant location make it perfect for both trekking and stargazing. The view of the lake beneath the stars is very breathtaking.

Little Spokane River Natural Area.

This natural region provides a tranquil environment for stargazing. The mix of woodland regions and river vistas can create a tranquil setting for your night trek. The minimal light pollution in this location increases your chances of seeing more stars and celestial objects.

Dishman Hills Natural Area.

Dishman Hills features various observation locations ideal for astronomy. The park's higher heights and lack of artificial light make it an ideal place for viewing the night sky. Explore the paths to find a comfy position with a good view of the horizon.

Beacon Hill

Beacon Hill provides a variety of hard walks and excellent astronomy chances. The height affords a wonderful view of the night sky, and there is less light pollution, making it easier to see stars. Find a good place on the slope with an uninterrupted view.

Spokane's South Hill

The South Hill region, albeit more urban, offers various paths that provide good stargazing possibilities. To see the stars more clearly, go to higher elevation sites or parks away from city lights.

Manito Park.

Manito Park, with its flowers and open areas, may provide an ideal backdrop for stargazing. While it's closer to the city, the park's wider areas nevertheless offer a good view of the night sky.

Mount Kit Carson.

Mount Kit Carson, located little further from Spokane, provides amazing astronomy possibilities. The trek to the summit offers a spectacular view of the night sky and a stunning background for your stargazing adventure.

Best Gear for Night Hiking

When it comes to night hiking and stargazing, having the proper equipment may make all the difference. Here's a comprehensive list of required and suggested gear for a safe and pleasurable midnight adventure:

Headlamp or flashlight.

A high-quality headlamp or flashlight is necessary. Choose a headlight with adjustable brightness and a red light option to protect your night vision. Make sure you have additional batteries or a backup light source in case the main light fails.

Reflective clothing.

Wear fluorescent clothes or accessories to improve your visibility. Reflective vests or strips can help people find you in low-light situations, particularly if you're hiking near roads or busy routes.

Warm clothing.

Even in the summer, temperatures can drop dramatically at night. Bring warm layers, such as a lightweight, insulated jacket, hat, and gloves, to remain warm when temperatures drop.

Navigation Tools.

Bring a map and compass as backup navigation equipment. GPS gadgets are useful, but they may fail or run out of battery. Knowing how to use a map and compass can help you navigate in the dark.

Prepare an emergency kit with essential goods such as a first aid kit, multi-tool, whistle, and fire-starting supplies. Make sure your stuff is easily accessible and stored in a robust, waterproof bag.

Use an insulated water bottle to stay hydrated during the night. If you're hiking in chilly weather, bring an insulated water bottle to keep your drink warm and avoid freezing.

Pack additional snacks and energy goods. Night hiking may be physically hard, so bringing extra food might help keep your energy levels up. Choose high-energy, readily digested foods.

Camera or smartphone.

If you intend to do any night photography or astronomy, bring a camera or smartphone with manual settings. A tripod is handy for taking long-exposure photos of the night sky.

Trekking poles

Trekking poles can give additional stability and support on uneven terrain, which is especially important while trekking at night. They can also assist to relieve tension on your knees and joints.

Personal Identification.

Bring personal identification, such as an ID card or a driver's license. In the event of an emergency, having identification on hand can assist rescuers or authorities in rapidly identifying you.

Night hiking and stargazing provide an entirely other approach to enjoy the outdoors. The serenity of a nocturnal trek, along with the splendor of the starry sky, may produce powerful feelings of calm and awe. You may have a safe and fun night hike if you follow safety rules, choose the correct paths, and bring the essential supplies.

As you begin on your nocturnal activities, remember to appreciate the particular beauty of the night. The paths and sky change under the cover of darkness, providing new vistas and chances for exploration. So, pack your kit, plan your route, and prepare to experience the romance of hiking and astronomy. Happy journeys, and may your evenings be full of stars and peace!

CHAPTER 22

THE HIKER'S JOURNAL
AND TRACKING
PROGRESS

Many experienced hikers, including myself, believe that the trip does not cease after the hike is over. There's something really fulfilling about chronicling your experiences and development. It not only allows you to reflect on the routes you've completed, but it also gives significant information that may be used to future treks. In this chapter, we will look at how to keep a hiking notebook, monitor your pathways and experiences, and reflect on your hike. Grab a cup of coffee, relax back, and see how these techniques may improve your hiking experiences.

Keep a Hiking Journal

Keeping a hiking notebook entails more than simply writing down where you've gone. It's about capturing the spirit of your experiences, both highs and lows, and everything in between. Here's how to get started and get the most out of your hiking journal:

Choose your journal.

Your hiking notebook can be as basic or as detailed as you choose. Some hikers use traditional notebooks, while others use digital apps. Personally, I enjoy the tactile feel of a well-bound journal and the ability to make notes in my own handwriting. However, digital diaries offer several advantages, such quick searching, sharing, and cloud backups. Choose what best fits your style and demands.

Begin with Basic Information.

Begin each record with the following information: date, trail name, location, weather conditions, and companions. This knowledge offers context and allows you to recall things later. Like the following: "June 12, 2024, Mount Spokane, sunny with a light breeze, hiked with Sarah and Jake."

Describe the trail.

Go beyond the basic statistics. Describe the trail's characteristics, including geography, height fluctuations, and important landmarks. Was it a strenuous climb or a pleasant walk? Did you come across any distinctive flora or fauna? Include your thoughts and feelings on the path. This helps to create a vivid picture of the hike for later reference.

Record Your Thoughts and Emotions.

A hiking diary is about more than simply the physical components of the journey; it also serves as a place to record your thoughts and emotions. Were you excited by the amazing view? Have you had any personal trials or triumphs? Writing down these events can help your diary become a rich and personal chronicle of your hiking adventures.

Include sketches and photographs.

Include doodles or images in your diary if you're artistic or just like to personalize it. A quick drawing of a breathtaking view or a photograph of a particularly memorable location might improve your submissions and add visual context. I frequently find that a few drawings may express the essence of a scene more effectively than words alone.

Record improvements and lessons learned.

Think on what worked well and what may be improved. Did you acquire a new technique or find a better method to navigate a difficult portion of the trail? Taking note of these lessons will help you improve your hiking skills and make future journeys more pleasurable.

Track your progress.

Your diary might also be a record of your development. Keep track of the number of trails you've completed, your average trek time, and any personal achievements. This may be quite motivating and give you a sense of success as you reflect on your trip.

Tracking Trails and Experiences

Tracking your paths and experiences entails more than simply recording your travels. It is about keeping a detailed record that allows you to track your progress, revisit favorite routes, and establish new goals. Here's how to efficiently log your hiking activities:

Create a trail log.

Keep a thorough trail log in which you record information from each trek. Enter the date, trail name, distance, length, and difficulty level. Make note of any notable observations, such as wildlife sightings, weather conditions, or personal musings. A organized record allows you to keep track of your hiking stats and patterns.

Use GPS and applications.

Many hikers use GPS gadgets or smartphone applications to track their routes. These tools can track your journey, mileage, elevation gain, and other details. Apps like AllTrails, Gaia GPS, and Strava are ideal for this purpose. You may also combine these digital logs with your diary to create a more complete record.

Set and track goals.

Set precise hiking goals, such as completing a given number of trails, covering a certain distance, or taking on more difficult walks. Keep track of your progress toward these goals in your diary. Seeing your accomplishments in paper may be extremely motivating and help you stay focused.

Document personal achievements.

Document any personal accomplishments or milestones, such as overcoming a particularly difficult path, finishing a long-distance trip, or gaining substantial height. Celebrating these triumphs in your notebook can boost your confidence and enthusiasm for future treks.

Provide trail ratings and recommendations.

After each trek, consider giving the path a personal rating based on characteristics such as difficulty, scenery, and overall experience. This might be useful for future reference and exchanging tips with other hikers. You might also scribble down any recommendations or advice for others who might be hiking the same trek.

Reflect on Changes and Trends

Review your trail journal on a regular basis to spot changes or trends in your hiking habits. Are you drawn to specific sorts of routes or distances? Have you experienced any gains in your endurance or skills? Reflecting on these trends might help you understand your growth as a hiker.

Reflecting on Your Hiking Journey

Reflecting on your hiking experiences is an important part of personal development and enjoyment. It enables you to appreciate your previous experiences, learn from your excursions, and plan future walks with better clarity. Here's how to successfully reflect on your hiking experience:

Review your journal entries.

Relive your trekking adventures by reviewing your diary notes on a regular basis. Take notes on reoccurring themes, favorite paths, and noteworthy events. This evaluation process may be a great approach to recall and develop a better appreciation for your travels.

Celebrate your progress.

Celebrate your growth and accomplishments, large and little. Recognizing your successes, whether you've finished a difficult trek, increased your endurance, or discovered new routes, may raise your confidence and enthusiasm for future hikes.

Set new goals.

As you reflect on your adventure, make new hiking plans based on your experiences and interests. Perhaps you want to explore more secluded paths, climb higher heights, or join a group trek. Setting goals keeps your hiking excursions interesting and purposeful.

Share your experiences.

Consider sharing your hiking experience with others. You may publish blog articles, participate in online forums, and join local hiking clubs. Sharing your adventure not only helps other hikers find new paths and suggestions, but it also promotes a sense of community among them.

Embrace continuous learning

Hiking is a never-ending quest for knowledge and growth. Accept the lessons you learnt from each trek and apply them to future trips. There is always potential for improvement, whether it's in your hiking style, navigation abilities, or discovering new gear.

Reflect on Personal Growth

Consider how hiking has impacted your personal development. Consider how your hiking experiences have influenced your physical fitness, emotional health, and view on life. Hiking may be a life-changing event, and appreciating its impacts might help you appreciate the exercise more.

Plan future adventures.

Use your reflections to plan future walks and excursions. Based on your experiences, identify new tracks to explore, obstacles to overcome, or locations to visit. Planning future activities keeps your trekking experience interesting and thrilling.

Keeping a hiking notebook, mapping your tracks, and reflecting on your adventure are all necessary habits for any serious hiker. They enable you to chronicle your adventures, celebrate your accomplishments, and constantly progress as an explorer. As you explore new paths and activities, keep in mind that your hiking journey is as much about personal growth and memories as it is about distance traveled.

So, take your diary, begin chronicling your hikes, and enjoy the process of reflection and progress. Every path you complete, every view you see, and every lesson you learn contributes to the rich fabric of your hiking adventure. Here's to many more hikes, experiences, and reflections ahead. Happy trekking!

CHAPTER 23

PLANNING FOR YOUR
NEXT HIKING
ADVENTURE

Preparing for your next hiking trip entails more than simply selecting a path and packing your kit. It's about making objectives, discovering new places, and remaining connected to the hiking community. Having hiked several paths myself, I can guarantee you that careful planning may be the difference between a good trek and a forgettable one. So let's get into the stages that will help you prepare for your upcoming journey and make it all you've wished for and more.

Set New Hiking Goals

Setting objectives is essential for any hiker who wants to progress and challenge oneself. It provides direction, drive, and a sense of success. Here's how to successfully create and meet your hiking goals:

Reflect on Previous Hikes

Before setting new goals, take some time to reflect on previous treks. What did you enjoy the most? What challenges did you encounter? Did you fulfill your goals? Reflecting on these events can help you figure out what you want to do next.

Define your goals. Clearly

Your hiking objectives should be precise, measurable, attainable, relevant, and time-bound (SMART). Instead of generic goals like "I want to hike more," make precise ones like "I want to complete the five longest trails in the Spokane area by the end of the year." Clear objectives provide you a specific target to shoot toward.

Challenge yourself.

Setting challenging goals will help you push your limitations. If you're used to mild paths, try a more rigorous trek or aim for higher elevations. If you've always hiked locally, consider taking a multi-day trip or traveling to a different location. Challenging goals make the experience interesting and entertaining.

Break down big goals.

Large objectives might feel overwhelming, so break them down into smaller, more doable tasks. For example, if your aim is to trek a difficult path, divide it into stages: research the trail, train for it, organize the logistics, and then accomplish the hike. Small triumphs along the road will inspire you.

Track your progress.

Keep track of your progress toward your goals. To keep track of your successes, use a notebook, app, or spreadsheet. Seeing your progress set out may be quite motivating and keep you on target.

Celebrate Achievements

Don't forget to appreciate your achievements, no matter how modest. Each fulfilled objective demonstrates your hard work and devotion. Celebrating these accomplishments keeps you motivated and excited for future treks.

Discovering new trails and destinations

One of the most enjoyable aspects of hiking is finding new paths and locations. Each new path provides a unique experience and broadens your hiking opportunities. Here's how to successfully discover new paths and destinations:

Investigate potential trails.

Begin by investigating prospective new paths. Look for information on trail difficulty, length, and features. Websites like All Trails, local hiking forums, and guidebooks are excellent tools. Pay attention to trail reviews and images to get an idea of what to expect.

Consider various terrains and environments.

Don't limit oneself to a specific style of terrain or surroundings. If you've generally traveled through forests, try desert routes, alpine meadows, or seaside walks. Different surroundings provide diverse experiences and can help you improve your hiking abilities.

Seek recommendations.

Talk to other hikers, join local hiking clubs, or engage in internet forums to acquire ideas for new pathways. Experienced hikers frequently provide valuable insights and can recommend hidden gems or must-see destinations that you may not discover on your own.

Check trail conditions and accessibility.

Before leaving, check the trail conditions and accessibility. Weather can have a huge influence on trail conditions, so be sure the track is accessible and safe for hiking. Websites and local hiking clubs frequently give updates on trail conditions and closures.

Plan a Scouting Trip.

If you're exploring a new path, consider going on a scouting expedition to get to know the region. This might be a quick trek or a drive to the trailhead. A reconnaissance trip allows you to gain a feel for the terrain, identify potential problems, and organize your major walk more successfully.

Enjoy the adventure.

Exploring new routes entails accepting the journey and being open to new experiences. Expect the unexpected, whether it's a breathtaking vista around a bend or a difficult portion you weren't expecting. Each new trail enriches your hiking experience.

Staying Connected with the Hiking Community

The hiking community is a thriving and friendly network of people who share your enthusiasm for the outdoors. Staying connected with this group may improve your hiking experiences while also providing vital support and companionship. Here's how you can keep connected:

Join local hiking clubs.

Local hiking organizations are a terrific opportunity to meet like-minded people and go on group walks. Many groups offer monthly walks, events, and social meetings, which allow you to interact with other hikers and discover new paths.

Participate in online forums and groups.

Hiking-specific online forums and social media groups can be useful for sharing experiences, seeking advice, and discovering trail ideas. Joining these groups allows you to connect with hikers from all around the world while also staying up to speed on hiking trends and news.

Attend Hiking Events and Workshops.

Search for hiking events, courses, or seminars in your region. These events frequently include guest speakers, gear demos, and group hikes. Attending these meetings allows you to learn, network, and increase your hiking expertise.

Volunteer for trail maintenance.

Many hiking communities have groups dedicated to trail maintenance and conservation. Volunteering your time helps conserve trails and keeps them accessible and pleasant for everybody. It's also an excellent chance to meet other enthusiastic hikers and give back to the community.

Share your experiences.

Share your hiking experiences with the community via blogs, social media, or local events. Sharing your tales, images, and advice can inspire others while also adding to the hiking community's collective knowledge. It's a wonderful way to meet and interact with other adventurers.

Mentor New Hikers

If you have expertise and knowledge, you should try mentoring novice hikers. Provide advice, recommendations, and assistance as they embark on their trekking experience. Mentoring is an excellent opportunity to give back and develop friendship within the hiking community.

Stay informed.

Stay current on hiking trends, gear advances, and environmental challenges. Stay informed with hiking periodicals, websites, and news sources. Being well-informed allows you to make better judgments and keep up with the changing hiking terrain.

Preparing for your next hiking experience is an exciting process that includes establishing new objectives, experiencing new routes, and remaining connected to the hiking community. You may improve your hiking experiences and make each excursion more satisfying by reflecting on your previous experiences, setting clear and challenging goals, and connecting with other hikers.

As you prepare for your next trek, remember to plan ahead of time, remain connected, and appreciate the wonders that await you. Whether you're exploring new routes, reaching personal goals, or contributing to the hiking community, every step you take enriches your hiking experience. Here's to more paths, challenges, and great memories. Happy trekking!

CHAPTER 24

APPENDIX

As seasoned hikers, we know that preparation extends beyond just packing your backpack and choosing a trail. Having the right resources and knowledge at your fingertips can make all the difference in ensuring a safe and enjoyable hiking experience. This appendix is your go-to guide for essential contacts, navigational tools, further reading, and useful apps. Whether you're a novice hiker or a seasoned pro, this information will help you navigate the world of hiking more effectively.

Emergency Contacts

When hiking, it's crucial to have quick access to emergency contacts. Situations can arise that require immediate assistance, so being prepared with the right information can save valuable time.

Local Emergency Services

Spokane County Emergency Services: 911

For all emergencies, including medical, fire, and police. Make sure your phone has reception or consider carrying a satellite phone if you're venturing into remote areas.

Forest Service Offices

Colville National Forest Office: (509) 684-7000

They can provide information on trail conditions, closures, and forest alerts.

Mount Spokane State Park: (509) 238-4258

Useful for information specific to Mount Spokane and nearby areas.

Search and Rescue

Spokane County Search and Rescue: (509) 456-2233

They handle search and rescue operations and can be contacted if someone is lost or in distress.

Poison Control

Washington Poison Center: 1-800-222-1222

For any incidents involving poisoning, including ingestion of toxic plants or substances.

Local Medical Facilities

Sacred Heart Medical Center: (509) 474-3131

A major hospital in Spokane that can provide emergency medical care.

Deaconess Hospital: (509) 458-5800

Another key hospital in Spokane, well-equipped for emergencies.

Maps and Navigational Tools

Navigating trails can be challenging, especially if you're exploring new areas. Here's a guide to essential maps and tools that will help you stay on track.

Trail Maps

Local Hiking Guidebooks: Books like "Day Hiking Trails: Spokane & Northeast Washington" offer detailed maps and descriptions of local trails.

Online Map Services: Websites like AllTrails and Gaia GPS provide interactive maps, trail information, and user reviews. These can be accessed via smartphone apps or printed before your hike.

Topographic Maps

USGS Topographic Maps: Available through the United States Geological Survey website, these maps provide detailed elevation data and terrain information. Ideal for understanding the layout of trails and surrounding areas.

NatGeo Trails Illustrated Maps: These maps offer a balance of topographic details and trail information, useful for both navigation and planning.

GPS Devices

Handheld GPS Units: Devices like the Garmin eTrex series or the Garmin in Reach Explorer offer reliable navigation and the ability to track your route. These are especially useful in remote areas where cell service is limited.

Smartphone Apps: Apps such as Gaia GPS and View Ranger can turn your smartphone into a powerful navigation tool, provided you have access to a signal or pre-download maps for offline use.

Compass

Standard Compass: A reliable compass, like the Suunto MC-2, is an essential tool for backcountry navigation. Learn how to use it in conjunction with your map to orient yourself and navigate through the wilderness.

Trail Markers

Trail Signage: Always look for trail markers and signage along the trail. They provide valuable information about trail names, distances, and upcoming junctions.

Additional Reading and References

To deepen your hiking knowledge and prepare better for your adventures, here are some recommended books and resources.

Guidebooks

"**Day Hiking Trails:** Spokane & Northeast Washington" by Rich Landers: A comprehensive guide to local trails with detailed descriptions and maps.

"**100 Classic Hikes in Washington" by Craig Romano:** This book offers a broader perspective on hikes throughout Washington State, including some trails near Spokane.

Hiking Magazines and Websites

Backpacker Magazine: Offers articles, gear reviews, and trail recommendations. Their website is a treasure trove of hiking information.

The Outbound Collective: A website that provides detailed trail descriptions, photos, and reviews from fellow hikers.

Environmental and Safety Guides

"**Leave No Trace:** Principles for Responsible Outdoor Recreation": This guide is essential for understanding how to minimize your impact on the environment.

"**Mountaineering:** The Freedom of the Hills": While focused on mountaineering, this book covers essential skills and techniques applicable to hiking.

Local Hiking Organizations

Spokane Mountaineers: They offer various programs, classes, and group hikes. Their website is also a good source of information on local trails and events.

Hiking Terminologies

Understanding hiking terms can enhance your experience on the trail. Here's a quick glossary of common terms:

Trailhead

The starting point of a trail, often marked with a sign and parking area.

Switchback

A zigzagging trail that helps to ascend or descend steep terrain.

Elevation Gain

The total vertical distance climbed during a hike. It's an important measure of trail difficulty.

Loop Trail

A trail that forms a loop, returning to the starting point without requiring backtracking.

Waypoint

A specific location along a trail, often used in GPS devices for navigation.

Scramble

A type of hiking that involves climbing using both hands and feet on steep or rocky terrain.

Blazing

Trail markers painted or otherwise applied to trees or rocks to indicate the path of the trail.

Summit

The highest point of a hike, often a peak or mountain top.

Backcountry

Remote areas of wilderness that are not accessible by road and require more advanced navigation skills.

Water Crossing

Areas where the trail crosses a stream or river. These may require special techniques or equipment.

Useful Apps and Tools for Hikers

Technology can be a great ally on the trail. Here are some apps and tools that I find indispensable for hiking:

Gaia GPS

A top choice for detailed maps and navigation. It offers offline maps, route planning, and tracking features.

AllTrails

Provides trail information, reviews, and photos. It's useful for finding new trails and getting an idea of what to expect.

View Ranger

Offers GPS navigation, trail maps, and a feature for recording your hikes. It also includes augmented reality for identifying peaks and landmarks.

Hiking Project

An app that provides detailed trail maps, descriptions, and photos. It's a great resource for planning hikes and discovering new trails.

First Aid Apps

American Red Cross First Aid App: Offers step-by-step first aid instructions and emergency preparedness tips.

St John Ambulance First Aid App: Provides guidance on handling injuries and emergencies.

Weather Apps

Weather Underground: Offers hyper-local weather forecasts and conditions, useful for planning your hike.

Mountain Weather: Provides detailed weather information specifically for mountainous areas, which is crucial for hiking.

Portable Water Filter

Sawyer Mini: A lightweight and compact water filter that's great for filtering water from streams and lakes.

Multi-Tool

Leatherman Wave: A versatile tool with various functions including pliers, knife, and screwdrivers, handy for on-trail repairs and tasks.

Power Bank

Anker Power Core: A reliable power bank to keep your electronic devices charged, especially useful for long hikes.

Headlamp

Black Diamond Spot: A durable and bright headlamp that's essential for night hiking or emergency situations.

With the right resources, knowledge, and tools, you can enhance your hiking experiences and navigate trails with confidence. From knowing whom to call in an emergency to understanding essential gear and navigating the digital landscape, this appendix aims to provide a comprehensive toolkit for every hiker. Whether you're setting new goals, exploring fresh trails, or simply enjoying a day hike, being well-prepared ensures that every adventure is both enjoyable and safe. Here's to many more successful hikes and memorable outdoor experiences!

Map of Spokane

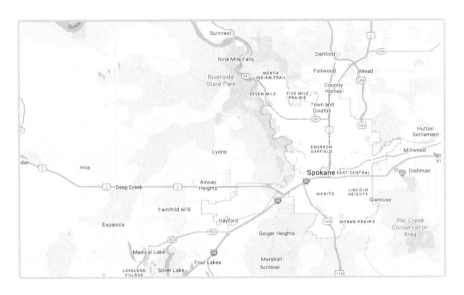

Scan The QR Code With Your Smart Phone
To Get The Locations In Real Time

https://maps.app.goo.gl/hGseNSBYQQHwRqu1A

Things To Do In Spokane

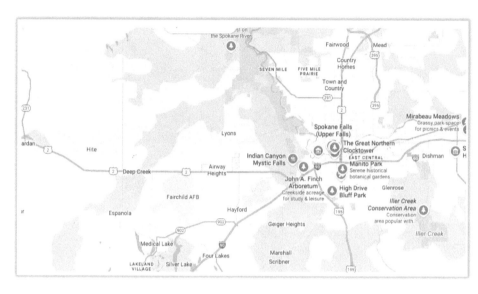

Scan The QR Code With Your Smart Phone
To Get The Locations In Real Time

https://maps.app.goo.gl/HhavQddT8R3cf9Pu6

Restaurants In Spokane

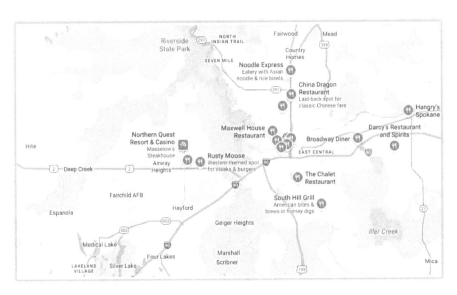

Scan The QR Code With Your Smart Phone
To Get The Locations In Real Time

https://maps.app.goo.gl/jSkHXzGFcwQih7Ww5

ATMs In Spokane

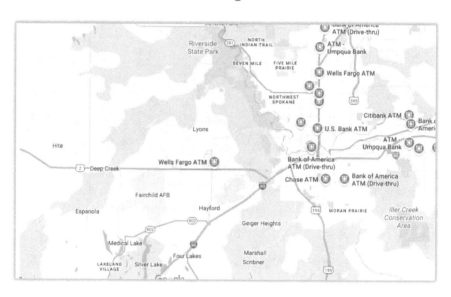

Scan The QR Code With Your Smart Phone
To Get The Locations In Real Time

https://maps.app.goo.gl/MySbvCBSCTLVigaa6

Made in United States
Troutdale, OR
04/05/2025

30347043R00130